THE
TABLE
STYLE
BOOK

First published in 1988 in Canada
by B. Mitchell

Devised and produced by Templar Publishing Ltd,
107 High Street, Dorking, Surrey RH4 1QA

Copyright © 1988 by Templar Publishing

Editor: Sue Seddon
House editor: Amanda Wood
Designers: Mick McCarthy, Robert Mathias
Typesetting: Templar Type, Dorking

Colour separations by J Film Process Ltd, London
Printed and bound by Motta, Milan, Italy

Canadian edition ISBN 0-88665-491-2

THE TABLE STYLE BOOK

JANE PETTIGREW

B. Mitchell

CONTENTS

A STYLE OF YOUR OWN

Whenever you move into a new home, or decide to re-style your existing one, a great deal of thought goes into deciding the use and style of each room. The size and layout of the house or room may not suit your plans. Sometimes the problem can be solved by major building or conversion work; sometimes your plans have to be modified to suit the house. Whatever your final decisions, they will inevitably be influenced by your life style, by the number of people who are to share the living space and by your budget.

Whether you are starting from scratch or redesigning, the dining area can be one of the most expensive rooms to furnish and equip. Mistakes may be costly, so it is worth taking time to establish the style you want. For those who can afford it there is the option of getting an interior designer to do the work, but if you are going to do the work yourself you need to plan the scheme carefully. You may already have some equipment, such as an expensive dinner service, which will dictate your scheme to some extent or you may have to buy everything. There is an enormous range of styles in furniture, china, glass and cutlery available and choosing a style can be bewildering.

Start with the room itself. If there is an existing dining room decide whether you want it to continue that function or whether you wish to convert it to a study or playroom and create a dining room somewhere else. Is it important that you have a separate dining room or

This dining area perfectly expresses the style of its owners. The overall impression is fresh and inviting with the white furniture, plates and table linen, pastel-coloured seat-covers, matching curtain pelmet and picture and the sparkling candle-holders and glassware.

Left: *The grandeur of these rooms is enhanced by the velvet chair covers and the coordinating dusty pinks and muted greens. The unusual marble table top contrasts with the soft luxury of the chairs and curtains, and the bronze cutlery also matches the overall colour scheme.*

Right: *This decor combines a stylish regency stripe in the wallpaper and blinds with the oriental feel of the porcelain and white slatting under the windows. The overall effect is of opulence and cool sophistication, enhanced by the rich detail of the lace table cloth, exotic lilies and fine china.*

would you prefer the dining area to be part of the living room or kitchen? If you are the sort of person who enjoys chatting to guests while preparing food, an open-plan kitchen/diner is ideal, as it allows you to be involved before and during a meal instead of being shut off in the kitchen while everyone else is enjoying a pre-dinner drink and a chat. If you are the sort of person who is easily flustered while cooking and hates people watching, you should probably opt for a separate kitchen if you can. If you entertain on a grand scale you may need a separate dining room.

When planning how much space you have for tables and chairs, remember that if your table extends with flaps and extra leaves, the room must be big enough to accommodate the extended table and the chairs and any other necessary furniture. If you have a large family you obviously need a big, flexible space to seat family and friends that may arrive unexpectedly for lunch, supper or dinner. Or if the size of your house or apartment limits the area you can organise for dining, a folding table and chairs may be suitable.

Once you have decided on the dining area you need to choose a style for it. This may be affected by the style of the building. You do not have to stick to the same period but in general it is not a good idea to mix styles. For example, ultramodern streamlined furniture will look out of place in a 17th century thatched cottage, and Regency-style antique or reproduction furniture will not suit a large space in a newly converted warehouse.

In most situations there can be no hard and fast rules since it is a matter of personal choice – what you like, what suits your lifestyle, what you can afford, what you feel best suits the house or room. The important thing is to have an overall plan and general picture of the style you wish to create before buying separate items. If you buy china, glass and chairs on impulse, they may not go well together. You need to think of the basic colour scheme, wall coverings, carpet, soft furnishings, lighting, the style of the furniture, the glassware, china and cutlery. They should suit each other, either because they are all made to fit a particular period, or because the designs and materials harmonise. Mixing interesting and even eccentric pieces in an individual way is often far more attractive and pleasing than a room that contains pieces that were made to go together and therefore looks a little like an uninhabited show-house.

Give yourself plenty of time to look around at what is available before buying anything. Wander round antique and second-hand shops if you are interested in period pieces, and take several trips to department stores to assess current styles. Keep an open mind – just look and let your eye adjust to the different styles available. If you can't visit department stores or shops, send for as many brochures and catalogues as you can. Buy magazines that show different interiors and list stockists. Take your time to formulate your ideas.

It may help you to think in terms of the categories of style that are available. These are the major alternatives:

Classic

Tables are antique or good reproduction laid with white damask, lace or plain linen cloths with matching napkins. Glasses vary greatly in shape but are generally cut glass or fine plain crystal of an elegant slim-stemmed design. China is usually white porcelain with coloured or gold rim, or ornate, elegant all-over patterning. Cutlery is silver or silver plate and shapes are slim and elegant with embossed handles or with initials etched into the silver. Knives may have bone handles that are square edged or slightly rounded. Candlesticks are silver, glass or china. Classic silver napkin rings also have their place here.

The overall feel should be one of opulence, elegance and refinement.

Traditional

Traditional wooden tables and chairs are walnut, mahogany or other mid-to-dark wood. Table cloths and napkins are coloured or white damask or printed, or embroidered with a pretty pattern of flowers. Cutlery is silver plate with simple handles, and glasses are cut glass but not over-ornate. China is floral or patterned with pictures, such as the willow pattern or similar, and the general mood is of comfort, well-being and solidity.

Left: *The striking black and white work surfaces, floor tiles, walls and units would look good with just one extra colour, but with this unusual china and bright flowers and vases, the effect is spectacular. The streamlined glasses and modern silverware blend well with the china and the geometric lines of the room.*

Far left: *This rustic dining room is simple and homely. Furniture is kept to bare essentials and is set off by the tiled floor and open hearth. For the table setting, earthy colours are echoed by the cork mats, wooden dishes, basket and earthenware casseroles. Herbs growing in dishes on the table are an unusual change from vases of flowers, and candles are simple and low-key. Stand six to eight candles together on a plate for an unusual display.*

The country look

For small country houses, cottages and farmhouses, the style is generally comfortable and charming rather than elegant and distinguished. Oak furniture is very suitable and table cloths are draped floral fabrics with perhaps a smaller plain over-cloth. Elaborate quilt work makes ideal table-covers for country homes. The china is traditional, fairly heavy floral china or pottery, the colours in the design picked out in fabrics for cloths and curtains. Glasses are plain and classic in shape, not too tall and spindly yet not chunky or solid. Cutlery is silver-plate, or bronze or pewter and of a simple, unfussy

design. 'Country' dining rooms give an air of calm rural life, and are rather pretty and quietly comfortable.

Contemporary

Generally colours are pastel or primary and shapes are simple with plenty of curves. Tables and chairs are modern pine, stained wood, hammered metal, chrome, glass or perspex. Table cloths, or mats if used, are simple plain colours or abstract prints in primary or bright shades. China can be anything from unusual shapes to very plain and curvaceous, brightly coloured or brightly patterned. Glassware is chunky and angular and some-

Left: *An unusual combination of styles creates a stimulating and bright room. The period fireplace keeps its strong character, but the modern paint effects on walls and furniture add an extravagant look, accentuated by the draped ceiling fabric that has an almost eastern flavour. The bands of colour on the curtains and table cloth cleverly break up the solid blocks of colour.*

Below: *The stripped wood of the chairs, table and dresser give this dining room a relaxed, country feel. Set for an informal lunch of bread and cheese, this dining set would serve a special occasion equally well, with the addition of a lace table cloth and stunning floral centrepiece.*

times frosted. Plain china or frosted glass vases and plain glass or china candlesticks are used to decorate the table. The atmosphere is one of light, colour and comfort without any fuss.

Stripped pine

Old pine tables and chairs are ideal for kitchen-dining rooms and give a feel of the solid continuity of life. The tables don't need covering with a cloth, but if you do use one it should be bright, checked gingham or single coloured linen. Mats are cork or rush or decorated with scenes from country life. China or pottery is solid and serviceable and brightly coloured, either patterned or plain, and of a traditional shape. Cutlery is simple – modern stainless steel with brightly coloured handles – or classic plain silver plate. Glasses are either plain and chunky, simple and curvaceous, or antique short-stemmed coloured glassware.

High tech

Tables for this industrial, mechanical look are hammered metal or chrome and glass. Table mats are black rubber or black, heat-resistant material. No cloth is needed and napkins are plain linen in stark colours. Cutlery is chrome or stainless steel and extremely simple and basic in shape – the only distinct shaping being for the fork prongs or the bowl of the spoon. Glasses are exceptionally streamlined with thick stems, perhaps decorated with bands of silver or black. China looks metallic and may even be made with a coating of chrome. Colours for the tableware are basic black and white or silver, or may be decorated with an all-over splash effect in a contrasting colour. Lighting on the table is several low candles or night-lights burning on a chrome tray or dish that will reflect the light, or a string of industrial-looking, clear, white fairy lights trailed across the table or in a glass or perspex jug or vase.

Left: *This light, uncluttered dining area is given an elegant air by the use of contrasting black and white, softened by the wooden floor, cane chair seats and light-coloured blinds. The china and glasses reflect the clean lines of the room, and the gently tapering candles are a perfect table decoration.*

Below: *Black accessories such as lamps, glasses and vase heighten the effect of this ultra-modern look and match the chequered floor.*

Right: *A feeling of comfort and security is created here by the dark, solid Victorian table, chairs and other furniture. The plain white ceiling is softened by the unusual use of dried hops strung across the central beam, toning well with the rustic lamp. The lace place mats, glass salt cellar and curved silver cutlery enhance the period flavour.*

Far right: *A delicate colour scheme of creams, greens and white give this elegant dining room a classic air. Touches of Art Deco style can be seen in the geometric chairs and chest of drawers, but the overall effect is softened by the use of flowers and frills elsewhere in the room. The table is set using the same colour theme, made special with a touch of silver ribbon round the napkins and a delightfully presented gift at each place setting.*

Victorian

Victorian tables were traditionally covered with white damask or embroidered cloths with matching napkins. Furniture is dark, heavy and solid. China is decorated with fairly dark designs of fruit or flowers, or country scenes, and cutlery is silver or silver-plate of a fairly simple design. The handles of spoons and forks are sometimes initialled and handles of knives are often bone. Glasses are coloured glass with plain stems and the table may be lit by solid, rather decorative silver candlesticks, often with octagonal pedestals. The general feel is of solidity and wealth.

Art Nouveau

The style, dating back to the turn of the century, is characterised by flowing lines and curves and a large degree of ornamentation. Art Nouveau tables and chairs are generally made from oak or mahogany. The china is decorated with a simple but flowing design and glasses have long elegant stems, possibly coloured, and curve

gently outwards towards the top. The handles of the cutlery are ornate and curvaceous, vases and flower bowls are often made from etched and enamelled glass. Candlesticks and candelabra are often made from brass, bronze or pewter and have a bulbous section for the candle above a slender, gently curved pedestal. To emphasise the style of the dining area, the room needs bronze table lamps with coloured glass shades in abstract patterns typical of the Art Nouveau period. Bowls, vases and other decorative objects may follow the designs of the famous glassmaker Lalique which typify the feminine curves and swooping lines of the period from 1890 to 1920.

Art Deco

The Art Deco period, from the early 1920s to the late 1930s is characterised by angular shapes and bright geometric patterns. Plates, saucers and dishes are often square or have acutely angled corners. Cups and glasses are sharply conical with zig-zag patterns and angular designs.

An Art Deco dining room needs simple fabrics and soft furnishings to set off the clean lines of the furniture and table accessories. It is possible to find modern fabrics printed with typical 1930s patterns that suit the style. Original china, glassware and furniture can be found in auctions and antique salesrooms, but they are often very expensive as they are now so collectable. It is a popular style, and china and glass manufacturers are reproducing some of the original shapes and patterns, or designing new styles to recreate the feel of the period.

1950s

As with the Art Nouveau and Art Deco styles, it is quite difficult to create a 1950s feel with new items, but if you like this period and are prepared to hunt, it is quite easy to find originals of the typical metal-framed chairs with wide curved seats, plastic-coated metal magazine racks and formica-topped tables. You can find china and glassware in simple curved shapes, often decorated in primary colours with pictures of fruits and vegetables, animals or flowers. Serving dishes are often asymmetrical, curved shapes, and dinner and tea services have plates, cups and saucers in six or more different colours. Table cloths are plain linen of a fairly heavy, open weave, and soft furnishings are printed in fairly dull reds and

Left: *A set of comfortable-looking leather Art Deco chairs and a beautiful table are matched by reproduction 1930s lights, candleholder, china and glassware. The colour of the wood is set off by the soft creamy yellow of the walls, creating a warm, welcoming atmosphere.*

yellows with black or grey texturing. Bakelite and plastic were used for cruet sets, ash trays, candlesticks, lamps and other items, and there are plenty to be found in junk markets and antique shops.

The overall effect is of a functional, practical environment with simple items that wear well and need little looking after. It is not really a style that appeals to a large number of people, basically because it was in fashion too recently, but it can be very attractive, and is particularly suited to small rooms where space for more ornate objects is limited.

Entertaining in your own style

The manner in which you entertain is just as much a matter of individual style as the decorative scheme of your dining room.

If you are worried about growing tired of your fur-

niture and tableware, choose a versatile style. A traditional dining suite in mahogany or walnut, for example, will probably blend with changes in curtain colours, style of carpet, new lamps and different china and glassware more readily than a distinctive ultramodern chrome-framed table and chairs. The more classic the style, the more adaptable it will be to different decors and houses.

Feel free to experiment and develop a style to suit yourself. You might like to give quiet supper parties for one or two friends at a time, or you may love cooking regularly for vast numbers of people. Whichever sort of person you are, don't feel you have to stick to what the etiquette books tell you. Today, the rules are more flexible. If you want to lay the table differently, if you want to decorate the table with a vase filled with vegetables instead of flowers, if you want to use an unusual fabric as a table cloth, then go ahead. If it creates the effect you want then be individual. The important thing is to plan ahead for each occasion. Decide on colour schemes, food, flowers, candles and special effects well in advance so that you have time to find all you need. Make lists of jobs to do, food to buy, decorations to make. The more organised you are the more smoothly the event will go. Of course, if your style is not to be organised, then there's no point in trying to change your character, but it does help to have thought everything out in advance. It means you worry less beforehand about things going wrong, you are more relaxed, and you and your guests enjoy yourselves more.

The yellow and white colour scheme and light wood chairs give a bright sunny feel to this dining room. The simple curves of the furniture and tableware suit the modern environment, and the softly draped curtains and generous displays of daisies provide a subtle contrast to the harder lines of the fireplace and shelves. The overall effect is of calm and harmony.

This striking dining room with its collection of furniture and decorative items creates a feeling of comfort, history and individual taste. The table and chairs speak of British baronial halls, the collected objects tell of foreign travels, and the windows, ceiling and wallpaper reflect a feel for traditional design and architecture.

SHEER ESSENTIALS

S o, you've decided on the style that best suits your taste – and your home. Now you need to invest in some essential items – a table and chairs perhaps, some china or cutlery? Choosing the basics with entertaining in mind needs some consideration.

Tables

Before you buy a particular style of dining table, there are several important practical considerations to bear in mind, beginning with the shape. The shape of the table will be affected by the design and size of the room. A round, hexagonal or octagonal table will fit well into a square room and often allows for more seating than a square or rectangular one. An oval table will fit happily into almost any area, and also allows for more chair space. A square or rectangular table does not necessarily need a particularly large room. It will look stylish if it does not exactly reflect the shape of the space – a square table in a rectangular room is better than a square table in a square room. When extended, square tables often become rectangular in shape so be aware of the maximum dimensions when making a choice.

Size is also important. Large, oblong tables that seat 12 or more people need an extensive room that does not cramp the furniture. Unless the size of the house or flat allows for this, an oval or round table is a safer choice. Large refectory tables are really only suitable for stately homes and mansions that have rooms intended for such furniture.

When choosing a table, take along a scale plan of the room for which it is intended, and a tape measure. Measure the possible table very carefully and mark on your plan the space that it would occupy. Does it leave

All the essential items chosen for this dining room are stylish and versatile, from the table and chairs to the classic white china and glassware. The black mats look effective against a pale table top but would also look good on a white or grey table cloth, or on dark wood.

enough room for chairs, sideboard and other furniture? Will the table seat as many people as you expect to entertain at any one time? Each person needs approximately 60 cm (2 ft) of table edge, so choose a table large enough to seat guests, but of the right dimensions for your dining room.

Take your time and try never to buy on impulse. Your basic furniture will probably have to last you for many years, so consider the quality and durability and its versatility. Spend time wandering around furniture stores to see what is available and what you like. When browsing through showrooms, ask for information about

the sorts of wood in which a particular table is made. Is it solid wood or veneer and chipboard? Will it withstand heat? How should you look after it? Check the quality by looking at joints and finishings to see the standard of workmanship. If you have any doubts at all, don't buy. Look for a similar but better product elsewhere.

Chairs

Chairs are often available as a matching set with the table. You may, however, wish to buy them separately for reasons of style or comfort or because you have found a table in an auction or second-hand shop. If you buy separately, think carefully about style and dimensions – delicate chairs with spindly legs will look out of place with a large oblong refectory-style table. Matching the wood is also important – pale beech chairs may look wrong with an oak table and dark mahogany often looks odd beside stripped pine or walnut.

The size of your table obviously governs the number of chairs that will fit round it. Each person needs approximately 90 cm^2 (35 square inches) to sit comfortably on, and the seat of the chair should be approximately 25-30 cm (10-12 inches) below the top of the table.

Test the chairs in the shop or sales room. Sit on one and rock it gently on to its back legs to see how strong the joints are. Do they groan and creak and feel as if they may give way? It is expensive to have joints repaired so make sure that they will last. Is the chair comfortable? Does the back dig into your spine or shoulder blades? Is there enough leg room to go under the table? Is the seat comfortable and sturdy?

The final question is how many to buy? Most basic sets of chairs are made in fours or sixes but you may decide you need more. If so, will they all fit into the room, around the table and standing in corners? If not, will they look attractive in other rooms as extras, in the hall or bedroom for example? You may even decide to buy folding chairs that will stack neatly into a cupboard until needed.

China

Your choice of china will probably be governed by the price you wish to pay as much as by design. Prices vary enormously from serviceable and attractive china at very reasonable prices in some of the chain stores, to very expensive dinner services made by the established

The chrome frames of these elegant chairs are well suited to the black and white scheme, and the rug under the table provides interesting detail. The unfussy lines of the furniture are echoed in the simplicity of the tableware. For variety, on different occasions, use a patterned table cloth or plain linen in a strong colour, and add candlesticks and a vase of flowers to match.

china companies. You need to decide, first, on the quality of china.

Do you want the very best bone china or porcelain, or would you prefer earthenware or stoneware or a cheaper grade of china? Bone china and porcelain are durable, as long as they are treated with respect, and, in fact, they chip far less easily than some pottery. However, china with any gold decoration needs very careful handling as the gold leaf may wear away very quickly if the china is washed in a dishwasher.

Pottery and earthenware are cheaper and easier to care for, and are more suitable for use in a microwave oven. You may decide that two sets are necessary – one bone china service for smart occasions and a cheaper set for everyday use.

If you choose a very expensive china, it is possible to buy it in sales or seconds shops. The pieces may be seconds but the flaws are usually so tiny that they do not notice. The only drawback of buying seconds is that you may not always find the particular pieces you need. Alternatively you may decide to look for a set in a second-hand shop or auction.

The design of the china you choose will be affected by the style of your dining room. If you plan to have an elegant dining room with a large table, silver candelabra and mahogany furniture, a formal, bone china dinner service will be appropriate. If you decide that an open-plan living-cum-dining room with a modern pine table and chairs are more suitable for your life style, choose a bright and serviceable set of stoneware or china from a contemporary store.

The stronger the design and colour of your china the less versatile it is. Plain colours, particularly cream and white, are the most versatile, and allow you to ring the changes by varying the use of flowers, table linens and table decorations. China with abstract or pastel floral designs is also versatile.

When you have chosen a particular design, your next decision to make is the type and quantity of each piece you need. For most situations you need large dinner plates, smaller flat dessert plates, pudding bowls which will double as soup bowls or cereal bowls, side plates which are also tea plates, two or three serving dishes for vegetables, a meat serving dish and a gravy boat. If you decide to have the same service for tea and coffee, you also need tea cups and saucers, a sugar bowl, milk jug, cream jug, possibly a tea pot, and, if available, coffee cups and saucers and a coffee pot. The quantity

Left: *This unusual brunch set is more limiting than a plainer design, but it is so eye-catching that it has an immediate appeal. Any of the colours of such vividly patterned china can be echoed in the table setting, and it looks best with simple stainless steel cutlery or that with coloured handles in a matching shade.*

Far left, above: *This graceful service would be excellent if you enjoy devising different table settings for different occasions, since the versatile plain white lends itself to almost any colour scheme. This design has the elegance of antique china and the touch of gold lifts it from being ordinary or everyday.*

Far left, below: *The classic floral design makes this china suitable for country houses and cottages, or for any interior where a traditional effect is wanted. The touches of gold make it special enough for formal occasions and the different colours in the design lend themselves to various colour schemes. Set it on a deep pink cloth or match the pale grey-blue of the leaves to candles, flowers and napkins.*

Left: *China with an attractive design is suitable for displaying on a Welsh dresser when not being used. This service would be perfect in a country-style dining room.*

Right: *The stylish black pattern on this china is based on a piece of embroidery done in the 1930s. The design of birds with exotic plumage amid flowers and tree boughs looks good in a smart black and grey setting with black lacquer furniture as shown here, or teamed with a white table cloth. The perfect accompaniment of black-handled cutlery would suit formal and informal settings.*

Far right: *Etched glassware blends well with most classic china. These glasses have been chosen to match the ivy leaf design of the plates and to echo the shape of the antique green goblets. The glass bowls, again selected for their leaf pattern, are a particularly good choice as they will serve as dishes for chilled soups, hors d'oeuvres, side salads, desserts or as finger bowls or flower vases.*

you buy depends on the scale on which you entertain, but if you buy one set in plain white or cream china it will blend with almost any other set giving you extra pieces where needed.

Glassware

As with choosing china, allow yourself plenty of time to look at what is available before deciding which glasses to buy. You need to decide whether to buy expensive lead crystal in a classic design that will not date or whether to settle for a plainer glass in a fashionable design to suit your decor and china. Whichever you choose, always ask whether the pattern, style and size are readily available as you may not want, or be able to afford, to buy the entire set all at once.

A full set of glasses contains anything up to 20 different shapes but as etiquette today allows for more flexibility you only need a few basic shapes.

Red wine – is usually served in a short-stemmed goblet – the idea being that as the hand encircles the glass it naturally warms the wine and the warmth improves the taste. A tulip-shaped glass is best for claret and a wider rimmed glass for burgundy.

White wine – is served in long-stemmed glasses so that the hand touches only the stem, and does not interfere

with the chilled temperature of the wine.

Champagne – should be drunk from tulip or flute-shaped glasses that help to retain the sparkle of the wine.

Sherry – should be served in small glasses, roughly the same shape as wine glasses.

Port and fortified wines are drunk from glasses that are similar to sherry glasses but have a shorter stem.

Spirits – whisky is normally drunk from straight-sided tumblers; gin and tonic and other mixed drinks are usually served in straight-sided, tall 'highball' glasses, the idea being to retain the fizz of the mineral; neat vodka and other similar spirits are best in small slim conical-shaped glasses.

Brandy – large balloon-shaped glasses are best, as the warmth of the hand encircling the glass warms the brandy and the aroma fills the glass.

Other liqueurs – as only a small amount should be served, tiny glasses are correct. They are usually a small replica of the wine goblet.

Cocktails – the most conventional shape is a wide conical glass with a long, rather elegant stem.

The list of essential glassware for any household can be limited to a set of wine glasses that will do for red or white wine, a set of straight-sided tumblers for beer or spirits that will double as glasses for water on the dinner table, some sherry glasses that will double as liqueur or port glasses, and some highball glasses for long drinks. The number that you buy of any type of glass depends on how many people you expect to entertain at any one time.

Decanters

Today, it is acceptable to leave wine bottles on the table, so carafes and decanters are not as vital as they used to be. However, you may prefer to pour wine into a decanter for use at the table. You may also like to keep sherry, port and whisky in decanters so that they look more attractive on the drinks tray or trolley. Decanters are available in as many different styles as there are glasses.

Unusual, original and valuable glassware can sometimes be bought quite cheaply in auctions, and in antique and second-hand shops. You may also come

Left: *Plain glassware in modern designs will suit most types of china and decor. Choose your glasses according to the type of entertaining you do most often.*

Right: *For a lunch of bread and cheese, why not serve the food on mini-breadboards, which look especially effective on a wooden table top. Emphasise the rural theme with dried oats or barley as a centrepiece and as napkin-holders, herbs and leaves for the floral decoration, and an unusual candle-holder of a bread loaf or a festive cake.*

across antique coloured glass that tones well with your particular china.

Cutlery

Your choice of cutlery, as with the other essentials, depends on the overall effect that you wish to create in the dining area, but it will also be governed by the practical aspects of caring for it.

Before buying have a good look at what is available and decide which design and style will best match your china and glassware. You also need to be aware of the different metals from which cutlery is made as they create different effects on the table. Silver or silver-plate reflect light well, and when teamed with cut glass, fine china and candles, the table looks festive and elegant.

Pewter is stylish but does not shine like silver. It has a duller gleam and is best teamed with heavier china or pottery. Bronze is very elegant and gives a warm glow to the table. Wood is more functional than stylish and is ideal in a kitchen-dining room or on a table set in the kitchen itself. Stainless steel is the most practical but is not suitable for formal settings.

Never buy cutlery without handling it carefully to make sure that it fits comfortably into your hand. Hold the different pieces to see how the handle rests in the palm. Is it easy to put pressure on the relevant areas? Is the balance acceptable?

The last important consideration is how much care the cutlery needs. Silver, pewter and bronze will need regular cleaning although modern polishes do prevent tarnishing for quite a long time. Bone or wood handles should not be immersed in water, as the handles will break away from the blade. This means that they are not suited to dishwashers, but pewter, stainless steel, bronze and silver are all dishwasher proof. Stainless steel is the easiest to care for but as it is usually informal you may decide to buy one set of stainless steel cutlery for every-

day use and a smarter set for special occasions.

Check with the retailer or manufacturer that the set you choose will be available in the future as you may not want to buy the entire set. It is quite possible to manage with a knife, fork and spoon per person and add more pieces later. You may be able to buy individual pieces or individual place settings. Canteens of cutlery normally contain six or twelve place settings.

Whether you buy all at once or build the set up

Below left: *This delightful setting shows how attractive a table can be when items are chosen for their compatibility. The touch of blue on the glasses echoes the gentle blue of the frosted plates and the plant containers, with the pale damask cloth and matching napkins creating a perfect background. The intense purples and pale* blues of the bulbs in flower add extra interest as an alternative to cut flowers.

Below: *The yellow and blue china creates the theme of this table setting with cutlery and linen chosen to match the colours and style. The angular handles of the cutlery are ideal with the modern simplicity of the china.*

gradually, the essential pieces are: meat knife, meat fork, dessert spoon and fork, butter knife, soup spoon, teaspoon, serving spoons and possibly a carving knife and fork, and a gravy ladle.

Other essentials

As well as a basic dinner service in your chosen design you may also need some extra serving dishes that will not look out of place with your china.

Large serving dishes

If you regularly serve such dishes as pasta, casseroles and curries, you will need large serving dishes that can be placed on the table. Glassware and white stoneware are ideal for this as they will blend with almost any

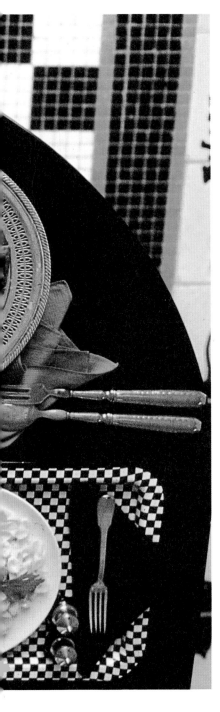

Above: *Don't be afraid to mix and match serving dishes to create a striking display. Set against a black table top, different bowls and plates team with colourful napkins in this eye-catching buffet. The chequered tray makes a smart addition, as do the celery leaves used to garnish food and dishes.*

Above: *A party atmosphere is conjured up by the glowing stainless steel serving bowl and dishes, the candles, coloured paper flowers, crackers and matching paper plates.*

design. They are also oven-proof and microwave oven-proof. If you stand such a dish on a dinner plate that matches the service, it will not spoil the table setting at all. The alternative is to find bowls and dishes that are so striking and individual that they become a feature in their own right. Check the heat-proof qualities of these before filling them with piping hot stews or soups.

Small dishes

You may also need extra small dishes for such starters as potted shrimps or pâtés. Little white ramekins are ideal for this.

Butter dishes

It is probably a good idea to have a variety of these for different occasions. For the kitchen – plastic, perspex, chunky glass or stoneware are ideal. For an elegant dinner table, little silver or glass dishes are best.

Gravy boat

If no gravy boat is available with the china you choose, one in silver or white china will fit with most designs.

Cruet sets

Chunky wooden or perspex ones are ideal in the kitchen or for informal meals. For formal dinners, silver, glass or china ones are best.

Salad bowls and bread baskets

Wooden salad bowls with wooden servers are ideal for informal meals. For a formal setting, glass is better. Glass or silver servers look best with a glass bowl. For bread rolls or sliced bread you need either a dainty basket or a silver or china dish to suit your dinner service. If there is no room on the table for a basket or dish, either place rolls ready on side plates or hand round as required.

Cheese board

Cheese can either be presented on a wooden board or on a flat glass dish or china plate. Scandinavian glass companies make very beautiful glass cheese dishes which are widely available.

Silver

If you regularly serve starters other than soup you will need cutlery such as pointed grapefruit spoons that can also be used for avocados or prawn cocktails. A set of

Classic design is teamed with modern marbling in this elegant dinner service. Here, it is set off by the rich fabric of the table cloth (which is actually a bedspread), the unusual silver candlesticks and serving dish, and fine glasses. The china would look equally good on white or grey table linen, a deep blue cloth or a chrome or hammered-metal table top.

fruit knives and forks with bone or mother-of-pearl handles are useful for dessert fruit.

For fish dishes, a set of fish knives and forks and possibly a large serving knife and fork are correct and attractive. A set of small pastry knives and forks is very useful – the knives can be used as butter knives at dinner or as tea knives, and the forks are essential for eating fancy cakes at tea-time. You may also need a set of coffee spoons that suit small, after-dinner coffee cups and, if your canteen or collection of cutlery does not include tea spoons, you will need some to double as egg spoons or jam spoons.

A soup ladle to match your table setting is essential if you serve soup at the table.

Candlesticks

Candlesticks are vital for central table decorations and your choice will depend on the particular blend of china, glass and cutlery. The size is as important as the style – small glass holders will look lost in the middle of a large formal dining table, while large silver candelabra on a small table obscure diners opposite.

Table cloths and napkins play an important part in creating an attractive table setting. Here, the colour scheme of the table cloth is also picked up in the plates, bowls, cutlery, vase, flowers, fruit and the unusual perspex chairs, creating a distinctive modern look.

Luxury extras

You might like to acquire some, or all, of the following luxury items, if you serve the particular items as regular features on your menus: artichoke plates, asparagus dishes, avocado dishes, corn on the cob dishes, oyster plates and snail plates.

Linens

Table cloths, mats and napkins play a vital role in creating an attractively set table. They can form the basis of a colour scheme or the basis on which a mood or theme can be worked. When buying linens there are some important considerations to bear in mind. Firstly, size: whether square or round, a perfect cloth should hang about half way down to the floor. Always take the dimensions of your table with you when you go to buy a table cloth. If your table expands remember to account for the larger dimensions and buy a cloth that will cover the extended table.

Secondly, the fabric: some fabrics are easier to launder than others. Damask and embroidered linens look wonderful but they do take more careful washing and more ironing than cotton or polyester-cotton fabrics. It is often a good idea to use an easy-care cloth and napkins for everyday meals and keep the more difficult or delicate cloths for special occasions.

Thirdly, colours and design: what will suit your room? The answer will depend on your china and the colour scheme of the room. Strongly patterned china looks best against a plain cloth that picks up one of the colours in the design on the china, or on a pure white cloth in lace or linen. Patterned china decorated in only two colours looks attractive on a cloth that uses the same two colours in a contrasting pattern. Plain china looks very effective set on a plain cloth in a contrasting colour – for example, black on white, yellow on blue, or green on red. Such contrasts are useful for special occasions that demand a particular colour scheme such as red and green for Christmas, black and orange for Halloween.

A patterned cloth is also attractive as a background for plain china, the design of the cloth echoing the colour of the china; white lace over a coloured cloth works well as a background for plain or patterned china. If you are going to buy an expensive table cloth take a piece of curtain fabric and, if possible, a piece of carpet and a small piece of china with you so that you can match the shades.

CREATING A DINING ROOM

Not all homes have a purpose-built dining room, and you may need, or want to use an unlikely space to create an interesting area in which to eat. You need not be governed by the conventional idea of a house with kitchen, dining room and living room. Look for other possibilities if your space is limited or unusually laid out. Creating such an area may require some basic building and decoration work or a complete re-fit, or it may just mean seeing the possibilities of an unused area and equipping it with suitable furniture and decorative objects. Such a space might be under a spiral staircase where space is quite limited, a conservatory, an extension to the back or side of the house, a basement, the end of an existing living room, part of a large kitchen, or in the hall.

There will also be times when you do not necessarily want to set a table in the dining area. You may prefer to set a tray and have breakfast in bed, or in the lounge or garden; you may like to eat breakfast at a special bench or bar in the kitchen, or you may set a quick meal on a coffee table or occasional table while watching television or writing letters. Whatever the situation, it is worth taking a little trouble to make your tray or table attractive so that your meal is an event, rather than a quickly snatched mouthful.

A delightful spot in dappled sunlight just outside the kitchen door makes an ideal place to take morning coffee or afternoon tea. The Indian table cloth, cane chairs, flowers, tall plants and grasses convey an exotic feel.

A table in the kitchen

If you have your dining table in the kitchen, the room must obviously be large enough to accommodate table and chairs for all your family and guests, as well as necessary kitchen equipment. It should be a table that you don't always need as a work surface or dumping area for cooking utensils. If possible, the table needs an area of its own so that, when you do sit down to eat, you don't feel that you are sitting amongst a pile of dirty dishes, laundry and other kitchen clutter.

The ideal solution is to have a utility area for such things as washing, drying and ironing, which will leave enough space in the kitchen for worktops, cooking equipment, fridges, freezers, and electric equipment – such as blenders and juicers. It doesn't necessarily have to be a streamlined, ultramodern kitchen, but it does need to be organised neatly and it needs decorative touches to make it feel warm and welcoming.

The kitchen should have a colour scheme just as other rooms do and you should follow this through the furniture and decorations. If you have a dresser, fill it with jugs, dishes, or plates, that create interest and emphasise the colour scheme. If there is no dresser, erect shelves to show off collections, if you have them, of favourite china, old cooking pots, or tea pots. The walls can be hung with pictures that relate to cooking or eating. Detailed colour plates from old cookery books or old, framed advertisements are absolutely ideal. Plants, flowers and dried flowers are just as important here as anywhere else in the home. Make the room feel lived in, warm and friendly and not just a functional area for cooking.

A kitchen/dining room

The difference between a kitchen/dining room and a kitchen in which you eat is that the two parts of the kitchen/diner are usually divided by a bar or unit of some sort, so that, although it is one room, there is a feeling of two separate areas which are furnished differently, have different functions and are separate entities.

The overall style, colour scheme and layout of such a room needs careful planning to allow for harmony and co-ordination – if the kitchen area is high tech in style and has matching equipment in chrome or black and white, the furniture in the dining part of the room should be in the same style. If you prefer old, stripped pine for your kitchen area, choose similar furniture for

the dining area. The colour scheme can be carried through in the blinds or curtains, the colour of the walls, accessories such as tins, storage jars, saucepans and other essential kitchen equipment. The dining area needs to have a softer, more comfortable and inviting appearance – cushion covers for the seating round the dining table, vases, pots for plants, lamp shades, picture frames. A carpet or rug in the dining area is homely,

Left: *This kitchen/dining room is separated from the main kitchen area by a handy breakfast bar. Used mainly for breakfast and informal meals, its sunny location is complemented by colourful chairs and crockery – guaranteed to provide a bright start to any day.*

Right: *One side of a spacious kitchen can be set aside as a dining area where linen and china are chosen to suit the informality of the situation. Simple china is all that is required, and mats are easier than a table cloth.*

whereas there may be tiles or linoleum on the kitchen floor. Lay the table with a cloth that reflects the colour scheme and choose china and glassware that is not too stylish or elegant but that looks pretty and smart.

A breakfast bar

If there isn't enough room in the kitchen for a full size table, there may be enough space to have an area which is just large enough for breakfast. This could be a table top that is bracketed to the wall and hinges up when needed, and hangs flat against the wall when not, or a slide-out surface which seats one or two people when fully extended and slides neatly away under the work top when not in use.

In a kitchen that has plenty of work tops, the third possibility is to use part of the work top area as a space for eating – either breakfast or informal snacks or brunches with friends. For this you need an uncluttered space that allows enough room for a couple of place settings and stools or high chairs to suit the height of the work top. If the work top is marked or not terribly attractive, then use place mats. Place a vase of flowers or a pot plant close by to jolly the setting up a little and, ideally, leave enough room for a folded newspaper or pile of letters so that the breakfast pots of marmalade or

Above: *A raised work top can also be used as a breakfast bar. The white tiles make a pleasing background for a calm and uncluttered breakfast, and a mass of tiny heart-shaped candles give a magical glow on a dark morning.*

Left: *Kitchen and dining room have been made into one delightfully spacious and sunny family area with pale green walls and plenty of plant-life providing a comfortable background. The colour scheme is carried through both parts of the room with plant containers, cushions and other accessories all contributing to the relaxed atmosphere.*

jam don't interfere with the morning's reading.

Your breakfast china should be chosen to fit into the overall colour scheme of the kitchen so that your nerves are not jarred first thing in the morning by unpleasant or clashing colour combinations. Breakfast should be a happy start to the day, so set the table flap or bar with co-ordinating cutlery, china and napkins.

A sitting/dining room

In an open-plan room like this, it is important that the two areas co-ordinate and complement each other despite their different functions. In particular, the furniture should be of a similar style.

There are several possible ways of arranging a lounge-diner. One way is to divide the room clearly in two and arrange sofas, armchairs and similar items at one end, and sideboards, table and chairs at the other. Another possibility, depending on the shape of the room, is to arrange the dining table in one corner with chairs around or beside it and other furniture fitted round the room as space allows.

Above: *The restricted space in this living-dining room is disguised by the white walls and ceiling, furniture and table cloth. A large mirror at the dining end of the room reflects the light from the window and gives an impression of more space.*

Right: *This conservatory becomes a successful dining area and uses all available space without looking cluttered. The narrow table leaves room for comfortable wicker chairs but is wide enough for plates and cutlery.*

If the space is very limited, the best option is to have a dining table that folds out of the way, and takes up as little room as possible when not in use, so that you can forget about it and use the entire room as a living room. Suitable tables are gate-leg tables and snap-top or tip-top tables on which the top tips up to rest in a vertical position against the pedestal. These then stand against a wall and take up very little room. Chairs for situations like this can be problematical; they either need to be very neat, and fit into inconspicuous corners or be stored in bedrooms or spare rooms, or they need to fold away and be stored in a cupboard until needed.

As with any dining space it is important to choose china, glassware and cutlery to suit the style of the entire

room, so that when the table is laid for a particular meal, colours, shapes and designs do not clash.

A conservatory

The great joy of a conservatory is that you can enjoy the sensation of sitting out of doors, surrounded by plants and flowers, natural light and the warmth of the sun (when it shines) without the wind or breeze to chill you. For this reason it is an ideal space for breakfast, lunch and tea, or for suppers in the summer when the light lasts well into the evening. If you don't have a purpose-built conservatory, a simple glass extension built on to the back or side of a room can create a similar area large enough to take a table and chairs and lots of plants.

For a garden room like this the most suitable style of furniture is wicker, basket work, cane or slatted wood. Make such furniture comfortable and inviting by piling it with cushions in a fabric that suits the theme of the room. Set the table for meals with pretty table mats to match the cushions, or cover it with a pale lace or linen cloth. Fill the room with plants on stands, in baskets and in tubs, hanging from pots on the wall and climbing up trellis work around the walls and ceilings. As an added touch, position an old umbrella stand, if you have one, in one corner and fill it with old parasols, umbrellas and walking sticks.

If the room needs electric lighting on dull days,

table lamps, standard lamps and subtle wall lights to fit the rustic theme are more suitable than overhead lighting.

For mealtimes, lay the table with old-fashioned floral china, use simple glassware and cutlery and decorate the table with a pretty china jug filled with garden flowers.

A space under the stairs

When using an unlikely and possibly limited area as your dining room, it is important to create an illusion of space and light so that guests don't feel cramped. White walls lit brightly by carefully positioned wall lights will help. Place a large mirror or mirrors on the walls to give the impression of an extensive room, and to help reflect and increase the light. Once the necessary dining table and chairs are in place, don't clutter the area with lamps or plant stands – a couple of pictures on the wall are enough to make it feel lived in. When decorating the table, stick to simple decorations – a white cloth, slim white or pastel-coloured candles to perpetuate the sense of space.

The choice of table and chairs is crucial – they must

Above: *A small corner beside the stairs has been adapted to make a charming dining area. Plain white walls use the light to best advantage and increase the sense of space. The clever positioning of a candle, burning brightly in a niche, adds more light without taking up valuable room. A lack of clutter, and pale cushions on the bench seating, add to the overall effect, transforming what could have been a wasted and ignored part of the house.*

Right: *A light supper is served in the casual comfort of the living room on occasional tables. The central table holds most of the food while glasses and plates are laid out on side tables. The vibrant colours of the flowers and pictures are repeated in the food, napkins and candles.*

be simple and take up as little room as possible and yet still seat guests comfortably. With some careful thought, clever choice of furniture and a few artistic touches, you may find that a space you thought was only fit for use as a broom cupboard will serve more than adequately as an unusual dining area.

Occasional tables

There are bound to be times when you don't want to set a table for a formal meal, but would prefer to eat casually while watching television or reading the Sunday papers, or perhaps even entertain friends to a late snack after returning home from the theatre or a party.

A coffee table, or occasional table, is ideal for such an event. The table can be set out as attractively as if you were setting a larger table. Don't just grab a mug and an odd plate, lay a place or places with mats, or even cover the table with a pretty cloth. Choose some pretty china and napkins and arrange everything attractively. You'll enjoy your meal much more and your digestive system will probably function a little better too.

If you are entertaining guests to a late snack or a quick lunch and the sitting room seems the best place, arrange the table with flowers or an attractive plant. Set a neat pile of plates ready with napkins and any cutlery you need. It is easier, in these circumstances, to choose a menu that demands a fork or fingers only. Trying to use knife and fork or spoon and fork while eating from a plate on a low table or on the lap demands a rather clever balancing act that can lead to disastrous spillages and a great deal of discomfort.

Before serving a meal like this, decide where people are going to sit and whether you will have to hand food round or whether people will be able to serve themselves. Also make sure that there is enough space for plates and glasses to be put down without the risk of being knocked over. If you decide to serve hot dishes or drinks, or glasses of wine, place mats on all wooden surfaces to protect them from scorch marks or sticky rings.

Eating from a tray

Trays are used when there is an invalid in the house, or when you want to laze over breakfast in bed or watch TV in the evenings. They are also used for morning coffee or afternoon tea either in the sitting room or in the garden on a sunny afternoon, or when you want to settle in a comfortable spot to read a book, answer some letters or just enjoy the peace of your favourite corner.

Setting a tray attractively for an invalid can be important, especially if a beautifully presented meal will tempt them to eat. Don't try to create an elaborate setting on a small tray, because there will not be enough room for decorative extras such as a small vase of flowers, or a tiny toy if the invalid is a child.

Lay the tray with a pretty embroidered or lacy tray cloth and arrange on it the basic cutlery needed to eat whatever you are offering to whet the invalid's appetite. Choose pretty china and never put too much food on a plate for a sick person – a small portion is much more tempting than a huge serving. Give them a large napkin as it is difficult to eat without spilling when propped up against the pillows.

The ideal equipment on which to serve food in bed is an invalid tray which has a top, a bottom and a side. The bottom rests on the floor, the side clears the bed and the top forms the tray. This leaves the patient's legs free to wriggle around without knocking the tray over.

Setting a tray for breakfast in bed is a quite different

affair. Choose a large enough tray to hold all sorts of luxuries such as smoked salmon and scrambled eggs, croissants, jam, honey, cream cheese and steaming hot coffee, or hot chocolate, as well as the necessary napkin, cutlery and newspapers. The tray should look as attractive as possible with co-ordinating china, tray cloth and napkin. The appearance of the tray will help the breakfast eater to enjoy the luxury of a short time of indulgence and peace, away from the chores and other demands of everyday life.

A reception area

There may be times when you want to offer a buffet meal or finger food with drinks in a reception area either at

Left: *This elegant tray is set with beautiful shell-shaped cups for an after-dinner cup of coffee. Placed ready on a table or sideboard with shell-shaped chocolates, decorative real shells, beside a matching yellow picture, the effect is impressive and visually appealing.*

Below: *A breakfast tray should look as attractive as possible. This china with its lively pattern will give a cheerful start to the day, and its colours are echoed by the napkin and fruit.*

home or in the office, or at a club or other meeting place. This will possibly call for the use of hired furniture, china and cutlery which may not be as attractive as you might wish. To make an area such as this attractive and friendly, rather than clinical and stark, use pretty table cloths to soften the decor, plenty of plants and flowers arranged both on tables and around the room and neat piles of brightly-coloured paper napkins that match the scheme placed ready on tables. It is crucial to arrange food smartly on attractive trays, with delicate garnishes such as mustard and cress, parsley and twists of lemon. Either arrange these trays around the room where people can help themselves or have waitresses or helpers take them round so that people are tempted to eat while chatting in groups.

TIME TO EAT

E ach part of the day has a very distinct character and atmosphere, and meals, table settings and decorative touches on the table should reflect the different moods. Breakfast should be light-hearted and fun; lunch should be a calm and relaxing break without any fuss; at four o'clock an elegant afternoon tea revives and refreshes; supper is a well-deserved rest at the end of the day and should be intimate, comfortable and attractive without too much decoration; dinner with a friend or friends should be stylish, elegant and as decorative as you wish to make it in order to create an atmosphere of harmony, warmth and enjoyment.

Breakfast

People seldom have time to eat a leisurely breakfast but when the opportunity does arise to sit and relax over a morning meal, it is worth taking the time to make it a pleasurable experience. Whether you are eating in a dining room, kitchen, conservatory, patio, from a tray in bed or elsewhere, choose a spot, if possible, that is sunny and bright.

Breakfast in bed

A classical setting needs a tray large enough to hold all the necessary items, which should be covered with an embroidered or lace tray cloth. The china should be a traditional pastel or floral design and the cutlery classical to set off the china. Fold a large linen napkin into a neat triangle or rectangle and lay it on the side plate with the knife, or knife and fork on top. Arrange food, the coffee or tea pot, a small milk jug and sugar bowl, and any letters in the spaces around the setting. In one corner, place a narrow-necked vase holding a single rose that matches the colours of the china, or simply lay the flower on to the tray cloth.

For a sick child, or for a fun start to a Saturday or Sunday when there's time to do more than snatch a quick bite before dashing off to work, choose really bright china for the breakfast tray. Cut a piece of brilliantly-coloured glossy wrapping paper that picks out a colour in the china, and lay it on the tray, and add further colour with napkins.

Above: *Breakfast tray settings should blend with the decor of the bedroom. Here, the black, red and yellow match the sheets perfectly.*

Left: *The glorious colour of the roses and the strong light and shadows of this corner of the garden set the scene for a relaxed and elegant breakfast. The shiny fabric used as a cloth reflects the sunlight and provides a clean, fresh background for the delicately-coloured china, the decorative glass apples and the glass bowls of fruit.*

For boiled eggs use novelty egg cups in the shape of favourite cartoon characters, or ducks or elephants, or use egg cups for jam, marmalade or sugar. Using food colouring pens or food colours and a paint brush, paint faces or bright patterns on to the eggs. Toast can be cut into "soldiers". For a child, lay a favourite comic in one corner, and for an adult a newspaper or magazine.

Breakfast tables

For a formal breakfast setting at the table, a cloth or table mats are equally good. Set each place with the china, cutlery and glasses needed for fruit juice, cereal, cooked food and toast. Fold large linen or paper napkins into fan shapes (see page 141), and place on the side plate.

Sugar bowls, milk jugs and jam and marmalade pots should match or tone with the china, and, if you have one, a silver toast rack is right with a formal setting. For a change from a central vase of flowers, arrange tiny bunches of flowers and foliage, to suit the colours of the china, into silver or porcelain egg cups and place one at each place setting. Alternatively, use spare bowls or jugs that match the breakfast service and place these, filled with flowers, along the middle of the table or at each place. For each person roll up a newspaper and secure with a ribbon about 4-5 cm (1½-2 inches) wide in a colour to match the setting, and place on each mat or above the individual setting at right angles to the cutlery. A touch of fun at a midweek breakfast can be created by placing a small clock at each setting.

It is important to get children to eat a good, filling breakfast before they race off and burn up masses of energy during the morning. So make a children's breakfast table as much fun as possible by using their own favourite, bright china with cartoon or story book characters, and choose paper napkins to match. As children often need more than one napkin, choose bright colours that look good together and either lay them down, one on top of the other so that about an inch of each one shows, or bunch several together and push into a mug or cup at each place. A paper table cloth is a practical idea, and if it's plain, children can draw on it with felt tips while they eat. Make sure that the surface underneath is well protected by an undercloth or an old blanket. Instead of serving conventional slices of toast, cut the bread into interesting shapes such as hens or ducks, stars or hearts, circles or diamonds.

Lunch

Setting the table in the dining room always has a certain air of formality, so if you want an informal meal with a friend or friends, eat in the kitchen, garden or living room. Lunch with a theme can be fun. Here are three which are simple and quick to create.

French wines and cheeses

For an informal lunch with friends, a selection of wines, cheeses, cold meats and pâtés, fresh fruits and salads makes a most delicious and attractive meal. To create an interesting and less conventional table setting than usual, give the table a French theme. As a table cover, spread out one or more maps of France. If you don't have maps, use strips of red, white and blue wrapping or crêpe paper, stuck together on the reverse. In the centre of the table make a flower arrangement in the shape of the French flag. To do this, use a rectangular, watertight container filled with a rectangle of plastic foam to hold the flowers. Use heads of red, white or blue flowers with about 1 cm (½ inch) of stem. Soak the foam with tepid water and gently push the flowers down into it, arranging them into three horizontal rows like the French flag. Use country-style tableware and place red, white and blue napkins around the table. Arrange the food on wooden or glass platters and let people help themselves. Leave bottles of wine and mineral water on the table to add to the informal, relaxed atmosphere of the party.

Fish and chips

A quick and stylish lunch can be created around fish and chips. Spread newspaper on the table instead of a table cloth. If you have a goldfish in a bowl, use that as a centrepiece. Eat the fish and chips from the packet or from newspaper. You can provide paper plates and knives and forks if you prefer.

Hamburgers, American style

If you are stuck for ideas for an easy, informal lunch, particularly for children, most faces will light up at the prospect of hamburgers and chips from well known chain stores. However, instead of turning the contents of the takeaway boxes out on to ordinary plates, you can make the meal a special occasion if you set the table with an American theme. The table cloth can reflect the colours of the American flag or feature a typical American motif such as stars and stripes, cowboys or Disney cartoon characters. Alternatively, use a large piece of sheeting on to which the stars and stripes can be drawn, or cut out of foil and stuck or pinned to the cloth.

If you want to use plates, choose disposable ones that fit the theme, or use plastic or kitchen-ware, or eat directly from the box or wrapper. Choose napkins to match the cloth and provide plenty. Fold the napkins into triangles and pile ready in the middle of the table for people to help themselves. Next to them, place a supply of knives and forks for those who want them. Alternatively, wrap cutlery inside napkins and lay at each place or in the middle of the table. Put sauce bottles and relish jars onto the table. If there is time, ask guests to come in denims, check shirts, stetsons and wearing toy guns.

Formal lunch

For a formal lunch choose a colour theme to suit the particular occasion and work around this to create a harmonious and co-ordinated setting. Pink is a particularly successful choice. To complement the pink you need a secondary colour to give depth and interest. White is an excellent foil to pink, as is very pale pastel green. Spread a plain white or pale pink cloth over the table, then set out glasses and china. The china should be plain pink in a darker tone than the cloth, or plain white. Alternatively, use china patterned with pink, or pink and pale green. The style of the dinner service and cutlery can be classic or modern, but the colour blend is crucial. Fold large, pink linen napkins into one of the classic shapes from

page 141 – the lily or bishop's mitre – and place carefully at the centre of each place setting. Fill an elegant
glass or porcelain vase with pink roses, white irises and
eucalyptus leaves, or pink carnations, pink and white
daisy chrysanthemums, and pink and white stock for a
centrepiece. The eucalyptus leaves or the delicate leaves
of the carnations blend well with the added pastel green
in the main colour theme. To finish off the decoration,
make small bunches of flower heads with very short
stalks. Fix the stalks together with wire or tiny elastic
bands, and pin the bunches carefully to each corner of
the table cloth, or space regularly if the table is oval or
round. However, if you are using very good quality lace
or damask, simply lay the tiny posies on to the cloth as
pins or stitches will damage the fabric. Before fixing or
laying the flowers in place tie curled pink and pale
green ribbons around the stems and leave them long
enough to hang or lay gently on the cloth.

High tea

The ritual of an elegant afternoon tea is an extremely
enjoyable one and, ideally, for the full atmosphere, tea

*Setting the table in the dining room always has a certain air of
formality. Choose a colour scheme to suit the occasion and
harmonize all the accessories. Pink and blue create a delightful
theme, and complement each other well.*

should be taken in the garden on a bright summer's day,
or in the living room in autumn or winter, round a blazing
open fire.

Tea from an autumn trolley

Tea from the trolley on a chilly autumn day is a warming
and delicious treat. Draw armchairs up to the fireside (if
you have one) and pull the trolley in to one side of the
circle so that the tea pot and cake plates can be easily
reached and handed round. Decorate the trolley with
wild berries and branches of old man's beard and horse
chestnut leaves. Use whatever china you have and bring
out the autumnal colour scheme with napkins in warm
browns, tans and ambers. If you have an open fire and a
toasting fork try toasting crumpets and muffins at the
fireside and sweet chestnuts in the embers. If you don't,
prepare all these things in the kitchen first, and bring
them in on covered dishes so that they keep hot. If you

are using a "real" fire, children might enjoy toasting marshmallows as well as the nuts and breads.

Mad Hatter's tea party

If you are serving high tea it is fun to have a theme that makes the meal more exciting than usual. One excellent idea is to have a Mad Hatter's tea party, where guests have either to arrive wearing hats that they have found or made specially, or to choose one when they arrive from a large selection of hats that has been thrown into a big basket by the door. The hats can even be passed around and swapped during the meal. The table itself should be a hotchpotch of ill-assorted china, none of which is meant to go together. Either use all your oddments from your cupboards, or raid the nearest charity shop for odd cups, saucers and plates. Introduce a zany feel to the food too, and make sandwiches with several layers and unusual fillings, decorate food with daft garnishes such as carrot tops, plastic or furry animals, liquorice curls, silly sweets such as dolly mixtures or sugar mice. Place napkins of all sorts of different colours under the plates and lay butter knives upside down with the blade pointing towards each person. Pour tea from a coffee pot and milk from the tea pot and put sugar into a milk jug. The madder the table setting the better. You really should start the meal with the sweet dishes and work backwards to the savouries, but only do this if you think the younger guests will still eat the more nourishing part of the meal as well as all the sweet and sticky dessert dishes.

Dinner

This is when you should pull out all the stops, indulge your fantasies and decorate the table in as grand or elaborate style as you like – depending of course on the specific occasion. For example, if you are entertaining an important business associate you probably won't feel that it's suitable to cover the table with pink tulle and drape swirling ribbons across and down the cloth. A slightly quieter approach is perhaps more suitable, but nevertheless, you need to be stylish. When planning any dinner party you must ask yourself a number of questions well ahead of the occasion and plan everything carefully. Decide first what sort of impression you wish to create – flamboyant, feminine, quietly elegant, floral, or high tech. Do you have a theme or particular event in mind. Do you want extra touches such as menus and place

Right: *Afternoon tea served in a charming cottage-style setting. The table should be laid with fine china and deliciously tempting food served on pretty plates. Guests should be given small tea plates and napkins and should be offered sandwiches or other savouries first and then scones or cakes.*

Far right, above: *This elegant tea is being served in a formal sitting or drawing room with a silver tea pot and sugar bowl, fine bone china cups and plates and crystal jam pot to add to the overall effect.*

Far right, below: *As an alternative to a conventional floral centrepiece for a Christmas or any other winter dinner, arrange alternate layers of seasonal fruit such as lemons or oranges, with doilies and fir cones on a glass cake stand. Choose the colours to blend in with your china.*

cards? Here are some contrasting ideas to follow.

Formal dinner

At a classic, formal dinner, flowers are a very important element in creating an attractive table and there are many kinds of arrangements that you can use to suit different occasions. Here are some alternatives to the conventional floral centrepiece.

Individual, small vases set at each place setting; try using Chinese lotus bowls or rice bowls, cocktail glasses, glossy, brightly coloured gift-wrap bags with tiny jars concealed inside, or small china or glass jugs.

Instead of placing the stalks of the flowers into a vase, use only the flower heads and float these in a glass bowl on a deep plate, in a silver dish or in wine glasses. For extra effect, add a few drops of food colouring to the water to tone with the main colour scheme.

Place a row of jars or vases in a straight line down the centre of the table. Try using a series of small spice jars or tall narrow-necked vases, a row of glossy, gift wrap bags in different colours and sizes, silver or ceramic goblets or beer mugs, unusual wine or other drink bottles, or a selection of antique milk jugs that blend with the style of the table. One or two flowers in each container should be sufficient to create the best effect.

Place one single, tall, striking flower, such as a lily, a gerbera, a poppy or an iris, in each of a row of single, tall vases and place along the table or in a circle in the middle of the table.

Pot plants make an attractive change from cut flowers; try placing a row of terracotta pots of hyacinths, crocuses, grape hyacinths, primulas, or snowdrops down the middle of the table. If you don't like the idea of the pots showing, hide them inside containers, or bowls, or

wrap each pot in crepe, tissue or gift-wrap paper in a colour to match the setting.

Lay tiny posies of flowers directly on to the table cloth, either in each corner or at random to fill gaps. Posies tied with curled ribbons can also be stitched or pinned to the hanging sides of the cloth.

Use flowers to decorate napkins or individual plates set ready on the table. Remember that flower and plant arrangements need to be kept fairly low – maximum height should be about 30 cm (1 ft) – so as not to interfere with people's view of each other across the table. Alternatively, the arrangement should be above the line of eye contact (minimum height about 60 cm (2 ft).

If you don't have any vases or you want a change from the vase that you always use, don't be afraid to improvise – try using an attractive tea pot, a milk jug, a storage jar

filled with coloured glass balls and coloured water, a copper jelly mould, a pumpkin skin, a goblet or a tankard.

Space age serving

As a change from conventional table settings, why not take space as the theme for a dinner party. This doesn't have to be a child's theme, it can be a highly sophisticated dinner for adults. Cover the table with silver foil or use a specially-bought length of silver lurex. If using foil over a quality wood surface, cover the table first with a piece of old blanketing or thick sheeting in case the foil gets torn and spilt food seeps through to the table top. To light the table arrange a string or two of white fairy lights across the middle or in one corner, or use high tech torches that are pen-size and give a very bright light. Arrange them so that the beams criss-cross on the table. Scatter silver and glass balls in gaps on the table, or use ping-pong balls sprayed with silver paint. Plates should be white, black or chrome and cutlery chrome or stainless steel. Use chrome-finish, high tech toys and decorative objects to decorate the table.

Farewell feast

If a friend or friends are emigrating, to Australia for

example, and you want to give a farewell dinner for them, you might plan a dinner around the theme of Australia. Either cover the table with a bright yellow cloth to represent the sunshine that the lucky people will soon be enjoying, or spread a blue cloth for the sea, and cut out a yellow outline map of Australia and stick or pin this to the cloth. For the centre of the table create a humorous talking point! Stick strong twigs firmly into plastic foam to represent trees and into their branches fix tiny, toy koala bears. Beneath the trees place some toy kangaroos to complete the scene. Make place cards in the shape of the outline of Australia or of the typical animals, and keep the table bright with yellow and orange napkins, yellow flowers such as Persian buttercups or double tulips mixed with soft grasses and ferns.

Make it a reunion

From whatever part of your life friends are gathered together, the essence of a reunion dinner is nostalgia. Decorations on a theme of school or club will work well for most reunions. Use appropriate old photographs (or their photocopies) as place cards for each guest, tie napkins with old school ties and use table lamps to light both room and table.

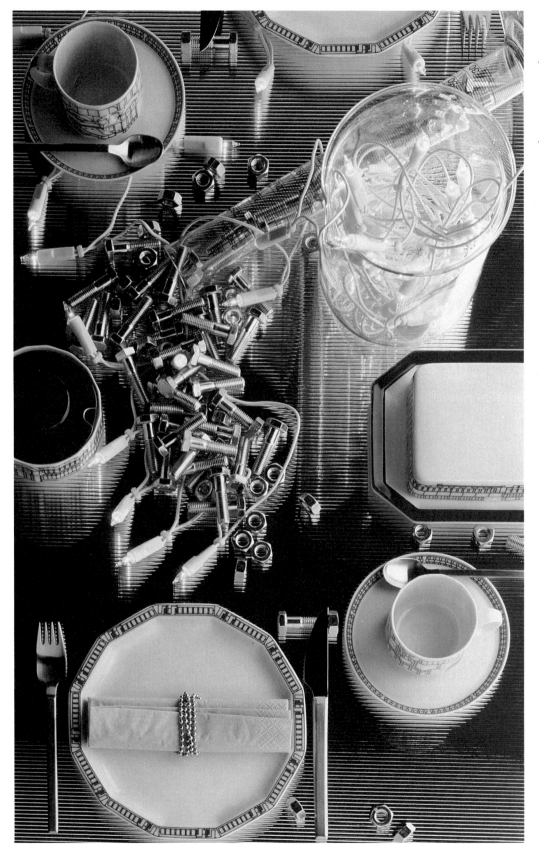

Far left: *This elegant centrepiece is easy to make: place tall, slim candles in rectangular blocks of florists' foam, choosing the shape of the arrangement to best fit your dining table. Insert sprigs of holly and other greenery around the bases of the candles to hide them and to cover up the florists' foam. Match the colour scheme of the arrangement to the colours of your table cloth and napkins: here, seasonal red and green have been chosen.*

Left: *A highly sophisticated space age theme, created by the imaginative use of nuts and bolts and fairy lights. The nuts and bolts are scattered casually over the table, picking up the pattern of the china and acting as knife rests. The fairy lights are arranged in a glass beaker, spilling out on to the table and twining round the nuts and bolts. The table's chrome surface reflects the lights, and the napkins are held in place with strings of silver beads.*

TURNING THE TABLES

With imagination and a little skill it is possible to take one basic set of china and produce a number of different moods and themes by changing the accessories, the lighting and the decorative touches used on the table. The most versatile china is plain white or cream because it doesn't impose its own character too strongly, but allows the other elements to work around it. When planning different occasions, don't be afraid to introduce unusual or unconventional, decorative objects which may be exactly right to set a theme, and may lift the table setting from the everyday to the highly individual and stylish.

Here are a few ideas for the sort of themes you can create.

Pasta and pizza

As the colours in the Italian flag are red, white and green, and as tomatoes and herbs feature strongly in Italian cuisine, reds and greens are the colours to use to set off white china and create an Italian theme.

Instead of flowers use a carefully selected mixture of vegetables and arrange them in a glass, white china or wooden bowl. Choose tomatoes, red and green peppers, celery, heads of garlic and bunches of fresh herbs. Polish the tomatoes and peppers with a little olive oil to make them glisten, and soften the effect of the rather solid shapes by placing leafy herbs in between them.

Large-leafed parsley or coriander are excellent for this.

The alternative to a central decoration is to place firm, ripe tomatoes of different sizes, and heads of garlic at random over the table. You may even be able to buy a table cloth, napkins and possibly table mats with a tomato design.

Pasta in various shapes and colours also looks very

Above: *Close-up of the central table decoration, with red and yellow peppers, artichokes, aubergine, fennel, garlic, and basil, all arranged in a white china dish. The shell-shaped pasta is placed in a large white shell.*

Left: *The Italian theme on this table is created by the red and green ties for the napkins and bread sticks, which are reflected in the colours of the centrepiece. Decorative pastas laid on the table cloth, olives, a black pepper mill and Parmesan cheese complete the setting.*

attractive as part of the table decoration. Fill little glass or white dishes with different types, loosely scatter handfuls of fusilli or tortellini on the table cloth or arrange coils of tagliatelli to contrast with tiny shells, bows, or coloured twists. Use a tall glass for grissini (breadsticks) or tie the grissini into bundles with red and green ribbon. Uncooked canneloni makes excellent and very amusing napkin rings. The table setting for an Italian meal is not complete without a huge black pepper mill – like those flourished by the waiters in Italian restaurants – and a dish of freshly grated parmesan cheese to sprinkle on the piping hot pasta or in the fresh minestroni soup. Burn red and green candles and play arias from operas, or Italian ballads to create the ideal setting.

Spanish style

Small dolls dressed as flamenco dancers or toreadors, figures made in Toledo metal, and colourful fans are ideal for decorating a Spanish-style table if you have them. Use them to fill gaps on the table between bottles of Spanish wine in raffia cases and colourful dishes of paella and deep fried squid.

The table cloth should be a strong red or rich purple to evoke the carnival colours of the clothes of bullfighters and flamenco dancers. For extra effect, lay a length of black lace down the centre of the table or wind it round your centrepiece. In the centre of the table place a bowl or jug filled with richly-coloured anemones or peonies. Tie black and deep red or purple ribbons to the stems

just below the flower head, curl them loosely and let them trail on to the cloth. Tie similar ribbons round the napkins, or fold large linen napkins into fan shapes (see page 141). Burn several coloured night-lights on the table and place lighted candles all round the room. The background music must, of course, be flamenco music and Spanish guitar concertos.

Below: *A Spanish-style table, with red napkins tied in black lace and matching night-lights.*

Right: *A close-up of the floral decoration, with Spanish fans and lace among the red peonies.*

Chinese feast

The colour scheme for a Chinese theme should be blue and white with bamboo as an extra feature. Basic white china is ideal especially if one or two blue and white rice bowls are added. Napkins can be tied with blue ribbon and chopsticks can rest on short lengths of bamboo. A bamboo rice steamer makes an ideal base for an oriental centrepiece of flowers and grasses. If bird of paradise flowers are available these make an ideal arrangement. Alternatively make a miniature Chinese garden in a shallow dish. Use plastic foam or earth as a base in which to stick a branching twig to form a miniature tree. A small mirror makes an excellent lake and stones or small rocks make mountains and give a distinctly oriental feel. If you have a small Chinese ornament – a little pagoda or seated fisherman – it will complete your garden. A beautiful bowl of floating flower heads also makes an eye-catching centrepiece.

Above: *A bamboo rice steamer makes an ideal base for a Chinese-style centrepiece of flowers and grasses.*

Left: *Blue and white is the ideal colour scheme for a Chinese feast. Use basic white china with blue and white soup spoons, serving dishes, tea pot and cups, all set on a crisp blue table cloth.*

Japanese minimalism

The typical Japanese table is uncluttered. Keep the setting simple – use a white or black table cloth, chopsticks and a plain bowl placed on a white dessert or side plate for each person. Napkins and place cards could be origami – the Japanese art of folding paper. In the centre of the table place a tall, slim vase with a narrow neck. Arrange in it two or three slender flowers – lilies or harebells – or a few elegant twigs of jasmine or apple or cherry blossom. As an alternative, use three identical tall, thin vases – black or white preferably – and place a single, long-stemmed flower in each. Place small bowls of rice crackers or sesame biscuits ready on the table and leave the rest of the space clear for serving dishes. Ideally the meal should start with each guest being handed a neatly rolled steaming hot towel. These are brought in on a tray and handed out with wooden tongs.

A typical uncluttered Japanese table setting. The white china dishes are an effective contrast against the black table cloth, with black and white napkins and black chopsticks. The beautiful shapes of the jasmine twirl around the three matching vases, creating an effective minimalist look.

Left: *Brightly coloured candles can be placed on a brass, copper or bronze tray to reflect the light. Stand the candles in gilt bracelets and strew necklaces around the tray, but be careful because you may get candle wax on your jewellery!*

Far left: *An Eastern atmosphere is created here by the gilded table cloth, metal dishes for chutneys and poppadoms, and the rich colour of the napkins, napkin ties and curtains.*

Eastern evening

Even if the Indian food you plan to eat has been ordered from a nearby takeaway, it is fun to create the right atmosphere by adding some typically Asian touches to the table. Lay the table with a paper or fabric cloth that is printed with a gilded pattern, or use an Indian cotton bedspread or large shawl. Set white dinner plates and side plates and the cutlery. Place glasses on little gold doyleys. If you have them, use brass and gilded dishes for chutneys, desiccated coconut and nuts. In the centre of the table burn scented candles in gilt candlesticks or light several small coloured candles in orange, red and yellow on a brass or bronze tray that reflects the light. Incense sticks burning around the room will heighten the Eastern atmosphere, and gold beads, chains and bangles strewn around the serving dishes add to the effect.

Traditional dinner

The table cover for a formal meal should be in white or pastel-coloured linen with napkins to match. A lace cloth placed over a plain coloured one, with napkins to match the undercloth, is also deal.

Alternatively use really smart table mats that tone with the colour scheme of the dining room. Plain, coloured mats with touches of gold are extremely smart and are often available in hexagonal or octagonal shapes as well as rectangular or round. If it suits the style of your room, a cloth that is generously swagged and tied with large bows can also suit a formal table and sets a rather more extravagant and flamboyant tone. There should be a second cloth underneath the swagged one,

Right: *Create an extravagant look for a formal table by swagging the table cloth and tying it with ribbons in bows. There should be a second cloth in a toning colour underneath the swagged one. The white, green and pink of this floral display matches the overall white colour scheme of the table.*

Far right: *A floral arrangement for a formal table must be the right height so the diners can look over it easily.*

the colour of which can be echoed in the bows and table accessories.

To swag the tablecloth, have ready either some strong, tight elastic bands or a needle and thread. Decide how wide the swags should be and gather the fabric upwards from the bottom edge towards the table top. When your hand reaches the edge of the table, bunch the gathered fabric together and secure with a firm elastic band, leaving a tight ball of fabric showing. Or, make several large stitches over the gathered fabric to hold it in place. Make bows from lengths of fabric that either match the fabric or tone with the colour. They are tied and then stitched or pinned into place to hide the ball of gathered fabric or the stitches.

Once you've completed your table covering, set the table with the white dinner service, elegant glasses and cutlery, and roll napkins that match the cloth into silver or glass napkin rings or fold them into fans or mitres (see page 141). For the centre of the table create a really special arrangement of flowers and candles using colours that tone well with the linens and colours in the room. Choose a shallow bowl or vase and fill it with plastic foam and wire. Have ready five or six slim candles in a colour to suit the cloth and napkins, and have a selection of slender and round flowers and some foliage. Decide on the overall shape of the arrangement and place a central tall flower into the vase, pushing it firmly into the foam. Then position the candles, spacing them evenly around the vase or bowl. Slim tapers will push easily into the plastic foam; with thicker candles you may need to tape cocktail sticks to the base of the candle and push these into the foam. Arrange the flowers and foliage to fill the entire space, using taller stems to fill the central areas and gradually bringing shorter stems towards the outer edge of the bowl, positioning them so that they lie almost horizontally. Dim the main lights and rely on the candles to give a warm flickering glow to the room. The overall effect should be of harmony, warmth and elegance.

Relaxed supper

In contrast to the elegance and dignity of the formal table, the setting for an informal meal needs little fuss or flamboyance. It should be inviting and relaxed but, never-theless, harmonious and attractive. An informal supper can quite happily take place in the kitchen, if the room is large enough, at an antique or modern pine table. If your table is less appealing in its bare state, cover it with a simple but colourful cloth. Choose a pastel colour scheme to suit the room, with a tablecloth in pale pepper-mint green, paper napkins in pale pink, pale blue and pale yellow. If you leave the table bare, use subtly patterned place mats in the same colours.

Set the table as usual, giving each person a white side and dinner plate, all the necessary cutlery and glasses. Fold the napkins into triangles and lay one of each colour slightly overlapping the next to create a rainbow effect on each dinner plate. The corners should point to the left. Alternatively, decorate the dinner plates with doyleys that are slightly smaller than the plates. Thread satin ribbons through the outer edge of the doyleys using either pale green, pale blue, pale yellow or pink ribbon to complement the colour scheme.

To decorate the centre of the table, use either a porcelain ornament that echoes the pastel shades, or fill a vase that repeats one of the colours, with a loose arrangement of pale yellow and pale pink daisies or carnations, pale blue scabious and stems of pale green foliage such as *Euphorbia marginata* or bells of Ireland. Alternatively use these same flowers, arranged in single colour groups to fill an individual container at each place setting.

75

The setting for an informal meal should be relaxed. Here, the attractive colour scheme is followed through in the table mats, napkins and flowers, and a rainbow effect is created by folding three different coloured napkins into triangles and placing them so they overlap.

RISING TO THE OCCASION

S pecial occasions need lavish table decorations designed to suit the celebration. They are opportunities to pull out all the stops and create a delightful atmosphere.

To celebrate an event with a large number of guests you may decide to hire a catering company to provide everything for you, which will probably mean that you will have a limited choice of china and glassware. If you organise and host the event yourself then you will have to plan every aspect carefully in advance: the guest list, seating plan, decorative scheme for the tables, the flowers, candles, china, cutlery, glass, linen and food. It is worth planning the details carefully: decide on any garnishes that you will need and make them in advance (see page 149). Make decorations and lay tables well in advance. You will also need time to iron the table cloth, wipe mats, clean and polish glasses, trim candles to fit candlesticks, fill salt and pepper pots and arrange flowers.

Place cards – If you are inviting only a small number of guests it is not necessary to make place cards to indicate where you would like people to sit. But for a large group of people you need a seating plan to ensure that you are in control of the mixture of guests at the table. It helps to put place cards with names at each setting so that people know exactly where they should sit.

Make the cards in a style to suit the theme of the meal. For example, if the meal is to be very formal, with an elegant table, use white card and letter in gold; for an

Left: *Silver and white is the colour scheme for this lavish special occasion table, set in an elegantly spacious room. Every aspect has been carefully planned, from the chair decorations to the matching table cloth and napkins. Contrasting colours are provided by the centrepiece of exotic fruit and the floral arrangements of gourds and other unusual plants; the twining silver-grey leaves hold everything together.*

Inset: *The addition of a gift, decorated according to the table's overall colour scheme, completes each place setting and heightens the feeling of luxury and extravagance.*

Easter meal cut the card into the shape of an egg or a rabbit and letter in bright spring colours. For further ideas and instructions see page 144.

It is normal practice not to seat couples next to each other and to seat male and female guests alternately. Try to place quiet people next to more talkative guests. At small gatherings this is less necessary as people will probably talk across the table as well as to their neighbours, but around a large table this is far more difficult, so there needs to be a good balance of guests.

Final touches – Before the arrival of guests take time to check the table. Is everything you need in place? Does the table look attractive? Are the flowers too tall for people to see over? Is the lighting right? Do you want candles alone or some wall lights on too? Would a coloured bulb create a more suitable atmosphere?

The final touch is the music. Do you want background music? If so, what sort? You may want to compile a tape of special music to suit the occasion – 1930s and '40s big bands for a cocktail party, romantic piano concertos for a St Valentine's Party, light string quartet music for a traditional dinner, and so on.

If you plan carefully and leave yourself plenty of time to organise, your party should be a total success which people will remember and talk about in the future.

Buffets

A buffet meal is ideal for a large number of guests at occasions such as a wedding reception or a large birthday party. It allows you to cater for more people, and it enables guests to mingle more freely, eating and chatting when they wish.

Where to place the table

If the table is pushed against the wall it leaves more space in the room for guests to move around, but it does limit the number of people that can help themselves to the food at any one time. This may not matter, but food, cutlery, plates and napkins should be positioned so that people can reach them easily while moving along the table in one direction or coming from each side. They can then help themselves without colliding with each other. Table decorations should be positioned at the back of the table, against the wall.

If the buffet table is far enough away from the wall for guests to move right around it, more people can help themselves at one time. Place duplicate dishes of food

Top: *A sparkling effect is created here by clever lighting, mirrors and glassware. The buffet food and drink are laid out on side cupboards which have glass shelves above and mirrors behind. Candles in glass holders and the glowing colours of the flowers, sweets and fruit enhance the overall look.*

Above: *This buffet meal is laid out on two adjoining tables around which people can easily serve themselves. The decorations are placed at the back, against the wall, out of the way.*

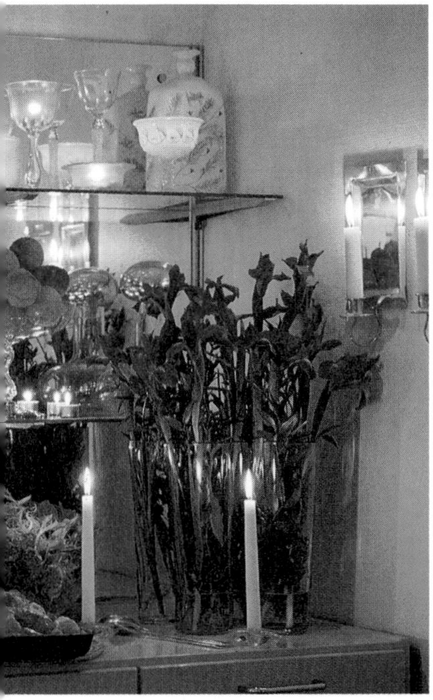

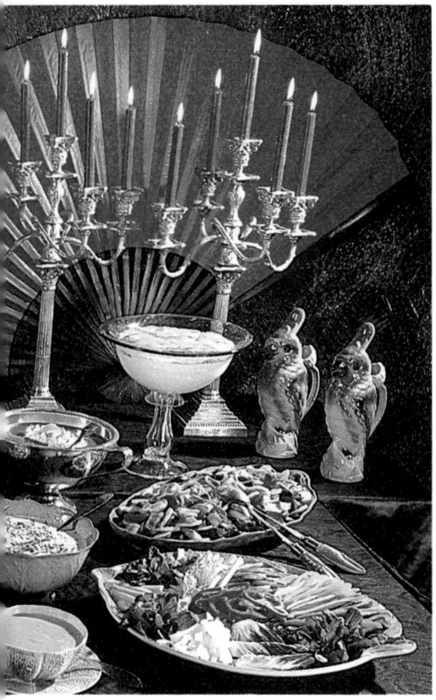

Where to place the buffet table

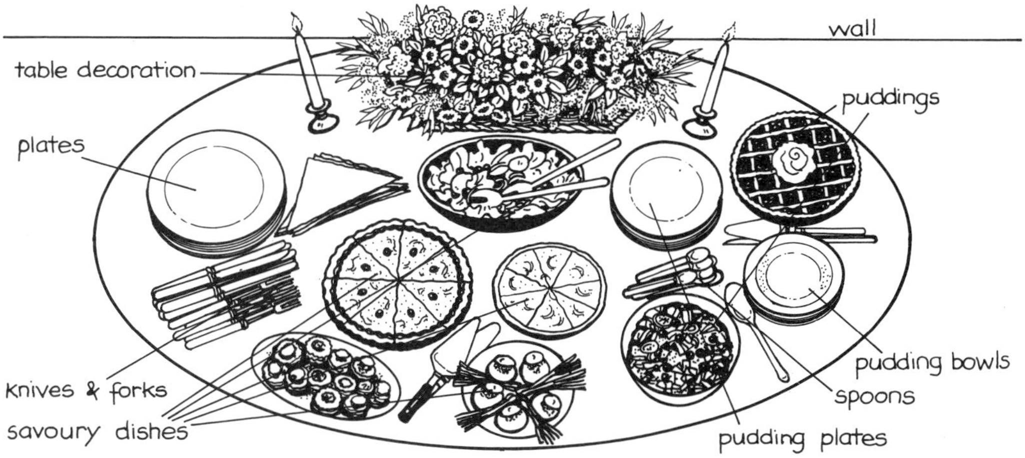
wall
table decoration
puddings
plates
pudding bowls
knives & forks
spoons
savoury dishes
pudding plates

Table close to wall

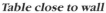

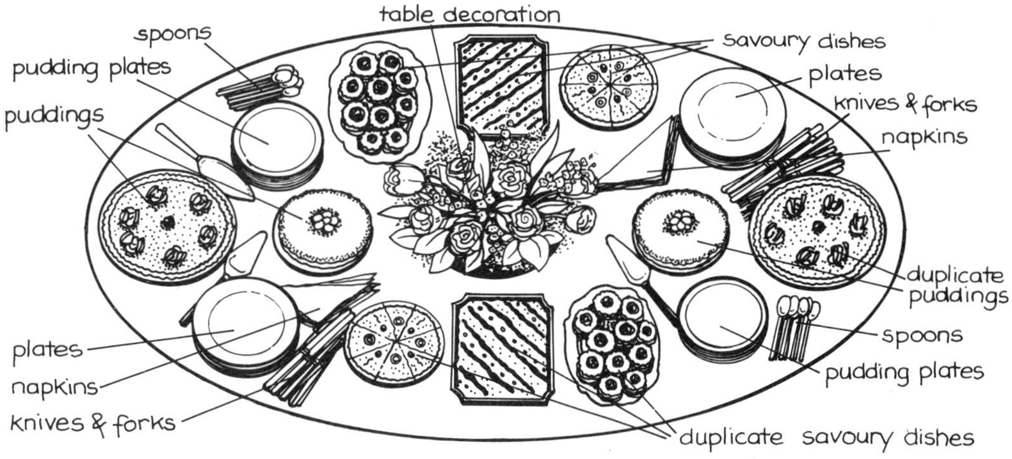
table decoration
spoons
savoury dishes
pudding plates
plates
knives & forks
puddings
napkins
duplicate puddings
spoons
plates
pudding plates
napkins
knives & forks
duplicate savoury dishes

Table away from wall

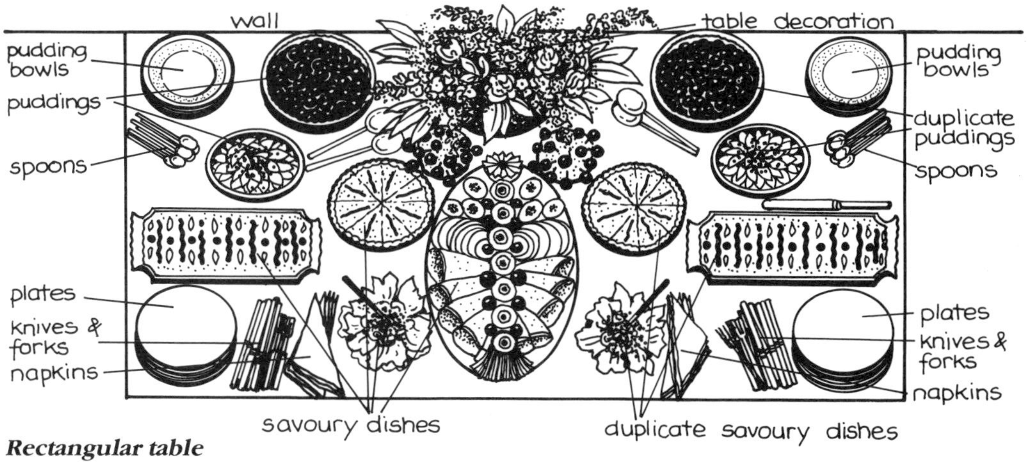
wall
table decoration
pudding bowls
pudding bowls
puddings
duplicate puddings
spoons
spoons
plates
plates
knives & forks
knives & forks
napkins
napkins
savoury dishes
duplicate savoury dishes

Rectangular table

and sets of china and cutlery on both sides of the table and keep desserts at one end, so that people who want theirs before others have finished the savouries will be able to get to the dishes without causing congestion. The arrangement of the table must look good from all sides, with decorations in the middle.

If there is a celebration cake, it is usually best to stand it on a separate table away from the buffet.

Christening

For a christening buffet, cover the table or tables with either pale blue or pale pink satin or silver foil and lay on top of this a layer of white net or linen. At intervals around the table, swag the top cloth (see page 73). Then, using wide satin ribbon in white, pink or pale blue, tie large swooping bows and fix into place with pins or thread at the point where the fabric is gathered. Arrange the ribbons so that they hang beautifully down against the undercloth. Into the centre of each bow fix a mock, white-feathered dove which can be bought in gift shops and florists, and use more doves to decorate the christening cake or as part of flower arrangements. These attractive paper and feather birds can be wired to the stems of flowers or twigs, or nestle at the base of a candlestick or vase.

Wedding

A wedding table should be very festive and elaborate, so use extravagant fabrics. Cover the table with either silver foil or white satin. Over this spread a layer of white tulle or lace or a net that has a silvery fleck. Gather the top cloth up into swags (see page 73) as for the christening table, or decorate the edges of the table with loops of wide satin ribbon in a colour to suit the bride's colour scheme. Pin the ribbons to the cloth at the top of each loop, and make generous bows to cover the pins. Leave the ends of the bows trailing down to the lower edge of the undercloth. Add to the bows streamers of shiny gift-wrap ribbon that have been curled and twisted. Use several streamers of mixed colours and tie carefully in amongst the wider ribbons.

For a more classic, traditional wedding table cover the table or tables with white damask or lace cloths, and decorate with looped garlands of jasmine, honeysuckle or ivy tendrils picked fresh from the garden. Measure the front edge of the table (or all the way round if it is to stand away from the wall), and decide how many lengths of foliage will be needed to form evenly spaced garlands

Above: *Beautiful hanging floral displays with appropriately coloured ribbons and white doves decorate a christening buffet table. Pinning sprigs of greenery around the table edge adds a finishing touch.*

Right: *This grand setting would suit an engagement party, wedding anniversary, 21st birthday or christening. The gold of the candelabra is echoed by the china's delicate gold rim, and crystal glasses teamed with elegant cutlery complete the table.*

along the edge of the table. The length of garland will depend on the size of the table but 100 cm (40 inches) makes a generously looped garland. Cut duplicate lengths of jasmine, ivy or honeysuckle and pin or stitch one end of the first garland to the edge of the table. Loop the other end up to a position that you have pre-marked with a pin to ensure even spacing and pin or stitch it into place. The next garland begins where the last one ends. When they are all in place pin bows, streamers or small posies to cover the joins. Tiny posies of miniature flowers with long streamers of narrow, satin ribbon look particularly effective. Use stems of the same flowers to trim the cake or cake board and to decorate the edges or handles of trays used to serve drinks or food.

Right: *For a Ruby wedding anniversary choose a red and white colour scheme, carried over into every detail.*

Right: *For a Ruby wedding anniversary choose a red and white colour scheme, carried over into every detail.*

Far right: *Create a dazzling, tropical table for an 18th birthday party in the height of summer. This exotic centrepiece of flamingo plants (Anthuriums), proteas and bird of paradise flowers adds the finishing touch to a table already overflowing with colour, from the brightly checked table cloth to the co-ordinating crockery.*

Ruby wedding anniversary

To celebrate any wedding anniversary it is an attractive idea to take the symbol for the number of years the couple has been married as the decorative theme – for example, fruit and flowers for the fourth, bronze for the eighth, pottery for the ninth, crystal for the fifteenth and so on (see opposite). Silver, Ruby, Gold and Diamond are the anniversaries most commonly celebrated.

For a Ruby anniversary choose a white cloth in damask or lace, and white lace trimmed napkins. Fold the napkins into heart shapes (see page 141) and lay on the side plates. Place a bow in ruby coloured ribbon on top. In the centre of the table place a classical arrangement of ruby red roses mixed with soft ferns and a touch of white gypsophila. Burn ruby red candles in silver candlesticks, and trail furled ruby red ribbons from each candlestick on to the white tablecloth. At the place settings of the guests of honour, place a ruby rose for each of them to wear during the festivities.

18th birthday celebration

Birthday celebrations for an 18th birthday often take the form of an elaborate party. But a formal dinner might be fun. Black and white makes a stunning theme and guests should wear formal black and white evening wear. Cover the table with a black cloth or black crepe paper that has been gently ruched and use white china, or set black china against a white cloth. Use white and black paper napkins and give everyone one of each, or roll white napkins into black ribbons, or black napkins into white ribbons. In the centre of the table arrange black artificial flowers in a white vase, or white flowers in a black vase. In the centre of the vase, place blocks of flower-arranging foam and push into this a piece of dowel, wound around with black and white ribbons. To the very top of this wand, pin or tie long streamers of black and white ribbons that will reach right to the lower edge of the

Wedding anniversary symbols

1. Paper	6. Sugar	11. Steel	20. China	45. Sapphire
2. Cotton	7. Wool	12. Silk	25. Silver	50. Gold
3. Leather	8. Bronze	13. Lace	30. Pearl	55. Emerald
4. Fruits and Flowers	9. Pottery	14. Ivory	35. Coral	60. Diamond
5. Wood	10. Tin	15. Crystal	40. Ruby	70. Platinum

table cloth. Trail these twisted streamers of black and white ribbon between the place settings. At each place lay a white or a black buttonhole which may be worn during the dinner.

21st birthday party

To celebrate a 21st birthday, you might take a theatrical theme and ask guests to come as well- known characters from the theatre or from a play. Prepare the room as the backstage area of a theatre with old sheets draped over furniture and props lying around. On side shelves and tables scatter masks, make-up, costume jewellery, crowns made from cardboard, copies of plays, and any other props that you can find.

Cover the table with an extravagant cloth (an old velvet or brocade curtain, or a richly coloured rug or bed cover). A model theatre would make an attractive table centre, or create an arrangement of paper or silk flowers entwined with a few feathers and beads. The idea is that these decorations should not look real but should add to the feeling of make-believe. Place a mask

or two on the table, and more costume jewellery, which can be tried on and worn. Set the table with the most flamboyant china and glass you have, or buy colourful plates and glasses from charity shops. Fold large linen napkins into one of the extravagant shapes on page 141-2, and set ready at each place setting. Organise the lighting so that the table is "spotlit" and becomes a colourful, central point in amongst the background of dustsheets and props.

Above: *A summery garden table setting for a 40th birthday tea party. Create an edible centrepiece from halved apples and meringue and continue the summery theme with miniature rose bushes as floral table decoration.*

Left: *Use chrome and glass, set on a glass-topped table, for a sophisticated 21st or 40th birthday dinner. Ribbon bows welcome each guest and match the gift-wrapped presents.*

Far left: *An unusual centrepiece for a celebration seafood supper can be created by tying a knot or a bow in a long piece of pearlised wrapping paper. Trail the paper across the table and on to the floor on either side.*

40th birthday party

Nostalgia is the key theme for a 40th birthday party. You might choose to celebrate on a theme of the decade when you were twenty or you might go for glamour and take the theme of Hollywood in the 1940s when glamour films were in their prime. Guests should dress in the style of the period or, better still, come as a star from those days. Decorate the room with some of the features of those early films – Art Deco sunbursts (which can be cut from cardboard and sprayed with gold or silver), feathers in vases or fixed behind picture frames so that they drape loosely, swags of gold, or silver beads draped across curtains and walls, tall plants and masses of flowers.

Cover the table with a length of satin, or with linen covered with a layer of tulle, in peach or pink or oyster. Roll napkins and hold in place with lengths of sequinned braid in a richer tone than the cloth. Under the braid,

Left: *Eggs of all shapes and sizes are the ideal decoration for an Easter tea. Add spring flowers and Easter bunnies, with a pretty table cloth and napkins, and garnish the food with edible flowers.*

slip a lily or spray of orchids. For the centre of the table, use a large Art Deco vase if you have one, or wrap any large container with silver or gold foil, or drape it with tulle. Fill with tall feathers mixed with exotic and flamboyant silk flowers, in the style of the head-dresses worn by Busby Berkeley girls.

Easter tea

For an Easter tea, cover the table with a bright yellow cloth and use white, or yellow and white china. Fold large linen napkins in green and white into rabbits' ears (see page 142). As a centrepiece fill a large, brightly-coloured bowl

Rising

RISING TO THE OCCASION

Left: *A warm earthy look suits a harvest or Thanksgiving table. Bare wood, dried flowers, grasses and fruits, pewter serving dishes and wooden-handled cutlery all create the right mood, and echo the seasonal colours of the food.*

with eggs – real painted eggs, chocolate eggs, sugar eggs, decorated wooden or papier mâché eggs or alabaster eggs. Place sprays of mimosa or jasmine around the edge of the bowl. Alternatively use a casserole or chicken brick which is made in the shape of a comfy, fat hen and give her a make-believe brood of tiny chenille chicks.

At each place setting arrange tiny sprays of daffodils, narcissi, jonquils, primroses and other spring flowers in egg cups or bowls. Garnish the plates of food, too, with flower heads. On each person's plate put a little chocolate or sugar nest of eggs or a rabbit or chick. Decorate the spaces in between plates of food with scattered chenille chicks, woollen bunnies and small chocolate or sugar eggs. For a children's tea, serve boiled eggs with faces or patterns painted on in food colouring, and serve sandwiches or toast cut into interesting shapes with shaped cutters – chicks, ducks and rabbits.

Harvest or Thanksgiving supper

To celebrate harvest or Thanksgiving, the table needs a warm, wholesome, rather earthy look. One way to achieve this is to use rich autumn colours – warm yellows and rusty oranges for the setting and decoration, and wooden plates, boards and bowls for serving vegetables, soup or cheese.

Lay the table with an amber coloured cloth and set rush or wicker mats at each plate and for serving dishes. Roll up rusty orange and deep yellow napkins, linen if you have them, paper if not, and secure in wooden napkin rings. Set wooden handled spreaders for butter, burn amber and deep orange candles in wooden holders, and fill a wooden bowl with polished, red apples and other fruits for the middle of the table. A vase or bowl (a hollowed pumpkin makes an excellent holder) of

Left: *Lighting is vitally important in creating the right atmosphere. For this romantic summer dinner for two, candles are placed in glasses and in hanging glass plant-holders and night-lights with flower-heads in a glass bowl provide side light.*

Right: *A single red rose is the traditional gift for a loved one on St Valentine's day, and looks effective brought in on this after-dinner tray. Scatter sugar cubes or flower petals over the tray to heighten the romantic mood.*

autumn foliage and berries will give rich tones to the table and will echo the golden colour of roast turkey, or vegetable soups and stews, and the red of cranberries served with the fowl.

An alternative is to use ears of wheat to decorate the table. Tie napkins with wheat stalks and wind others around candlesticks. Candles can also be fixed into plaited or knotted loaves of bread. First make a hole in the crust so that the candle will push in, and cut or break away as much dough as you need to make a firm candleholder. For an American Thanksgiving supper use miniature American flags as decoration. Place a knotted or plaited bread roll at each place setting and stick with a little flag. Use autumn foliage as a centrepiece or make miniature stooks of corn and arrange them in the centre of the table around the plaited bread candleholder. Serve traditional food that echoes all the colours of the season – pumpkin soup, golden roast turkey, crispy roast parsnips and potatoes, honeyed carrots, apple pie, pecan pie and lots of cream.

St Valentine's day dinner

This might be a romantic dinner for two, or it could be a meal for a large group of friends. Whichever it is, it should take as its theme the red heart. If it is a *diner à deux* the decorations should be quietly romantic – a vase of exquisite red roses in the centre of the table, red candles burning in white or silver candlesticks, your very best china and cutlery, a gift for your guest in a red, heart-shaped box, and deliciously indulgent food such as smoked salmon or caviar.

If the gathering is for a large group, it should be flamboyant and extravagant. Send out invitations on heart-shaped, red cards and ask your guests to "wear their hearts on their sleeves" by turning up at the dinner with their heart-shaped invitations pinned to their sleeves.

On the evening of the party, cover the table with a white cloth and decorate it with red hearts cut from shiny paper or fabric that can be stuck or stitched on. Make place cards in heart-shaped red card and write guests' names in silver. To liven up the proceedings write love poems on the place cards which guests have to read to another of their choice during the meal. Fill a shallow bowl with brilliant red roses and place it in the centre of the table. Scatter a few rose petals over the cloth around the bowl. Tie white linen or lace trimmed napkins with red satin ribbon. Have red candles burning in silver or white candlesticks and tie the candlesticks with more red, furled ribbons which hang gently down to the cloth.

EATING AL FRESCO

E ating out of doors is one of life's great pleasures. Whether you give a grand garden party, enjoy a family picnic, barbecue your supper or simply carry your lunch out to a sunny spot in the garden, food often seems to taste better in the open air.

A table in the garden

If you frequently eat outside, you may have a permanent site for tables and chairs. Or you may use fold-up garden furniture that can be arranged easily in a sunny spot when the weather allows. Wherever you position the table – on a patio or on the lawn – make sure that it is stable and that the legs are on even ground. There's nothing worse than a wobbly table that rocks every time you touch it and spills the drinks. If you choose a spot that catches the full glare of the sun, you may also need a large parasol or table umbrella for sun sensitive guests or when the sun becomes too hot for everyone.

In the evening you need to consider the lighting of the outdoor dinner table. If the table is positioned near the house, there may be enough light cast by indoor lighting to illuminate the dinner party. Alternatively, you need lights on the outside walls of the house, or lamps

A family meal in the open air is one of life's great pleasures. For a special occasion, decorate the table with masses of flowers, sugared almonds and tiny presents, and provide parasols for shade.

in the garden. If you have a big garden you may want to install flood lights that give plenty of light for all occasions. On a smaller scale, for special occasions, it's fun to string fairy lights or larger coloured bulbs along fencing or tree branches, or to burn garden flares which give a dramatic, flickering light.

The table itself can be lit with candles in glass containers which protect the flame from evening breezes. Coloured glass adds atmosphere by intensifying the glow from the candles. Lanterns and fairy lights are alternatives and can sit on the table, or be fixed to walls.

If you use a cloth on a breezy day use metal or plastic café clips (obtainable from specialist tableware and kitchen shops and department stores) to hold the cloth in place. They are particularly good for keeping paper cloths in position.

A party in the garden

For a special party in the garden, choose flowers and fruit as the theme, and decorate the table accordingly.

Place the table against a suitable backdrop – such as a corner of the garden where a flower border or climbing plants set the scene; beneath trees; near a pond, lake or swimming pool; or on a patio or veranda from which there is a good view over the rest of the garden. If the table has an attractive top do not use a cloth, otherwise spread out a large floral print cotton or linen cloth,

Left: *The fruit pattern on this table cloth is echoed in the bowl of summer fruit. If you don't have a table cloth long enough for a party table, use rolls of gift-wrap or wallpaper. Place the table in a suitable place for a meal, such as under trees for shade on a hot day.*

Far left: *This table is set for a lovely summer buffet party with the flower border and ivy clad building providing a perfect backdrop. The food is arranged so beautifully on the plates that it serves both a decorative and practical function.*

or use disposable cloths that have a flower or fruit motif. To stop the breeze from blowing the cloth away, use café clips to hold it in place.

To make a table decoration cut the top from one or more large pineapples. Scoop out the flesh and fill the hollow with plastic foam. Arrange ferns, roses, honeysuckle, daisies or dahlias in the pineapple shell or shells. You can also cut the pineapples in half vertically, scoop out the flesh and fill each half with flowers. The same sort of arrangements can be made using scooped-out grapefruit, melons, or pumpkins. If you are decorating a long table, use several fruits along the table.

An alternative idea is to build a cone of fruit and flowers, arranging rows of carefully selected items so that colours and textures go well together. First choose a suitable stand for the cone. You could use a glass cake-stand, a silver platter, a tray, a cakeboard covered with silver or coloured paper, or an elegant floral plate. Place on it a cone of flower-arranging foam, about 2.5 cm (1 inch) smaller in diameter than the stand. Arrange the first row of flowers or fruits by pushing their stems into the lower edge of the foam to hide it. Start, for example, with a row of pink dahlias or daisies, interspersed with ivy or clematis. For the next layer push cocktail sticks into large, green grapes or strawberries, and push the sticks into the foam so that the fruits rest just above the line of the dahlias forming a second ring. The third layer is flowers again, this time purple

Right: *Paper decorations with smiling faces set the right mood for this special garden party. The beautiful cream table cloth, swagged and decorated with flowers, is a fitting backdrop for the plates of summer food and the abundant fruit and flowers. Candles will provide light as the sun sets.*

Far right: *Roses are the theme of this summer tea, and the table has been carefully positioned in the garden for the best effect. Appliquéd flowers on the table cloth, rose-pink napkins, rose-patterned china and a hat with roses around the brim are extra-special touches.*

anemones or 'Devonshire Dumplings' interspersed with gypsophyla. Continue up the side of the cone, using alternate rings of flowers and fruits in complementary colours. The small space at the top can then be filled with strawberries, grapes or other small fruits, depending on the colours you choose. This sort of cone can be created using almost any fruits and flowers you have in the garden.

When serving the drinks at your flowers and fruit party, decorate the drinks with floral or fruit ice cubes (see page 153). Make the ice more interesting and colourful than usual by freezing tiny sprays of flowers, slices of stuffed olives, rings of carrots, fruits such as strawberries or raspberries, lychees, and grapes in the ice cubes. Make a frozen circlet of flowers, leaves and fruit by freezing strawberries, tiny flower heads and mint leaves in water in a ring-shaped jelly mould. When frozen, turn out the mould and float it in a bowl of white wine cup or punch.

If your party in the garden is a sit-down affair, add more colour to the table at each place setting by decorating napkins with sprays of flowers or place individual candles beside each setting. As candle holders, use apples or oranges, lemons or limes. Cut a slice from the bottom of the fruit to make each one steady and cut a small hole in the top for a taper or candle to rest in. You can do the same with baby cabbages, cauliflowers, large firm tomatoes or turnips for a vegetable theme.

Barbecue Country and Western style

If your garden is large enough and you enjoy cooking and eating outdoors, you may decide to build a permanent barbecue in a suitable corner or, if you don't trust the weather to make that worthwhile or you simply don't have the space for a large brick structure, you can buy small, portable barbecues that can be stored in a garage or cellar when not in use.

When using a portable barbecue choose a spot away from doorways into the house, so that there is no risk of accidents as people move from house to garden and vice versa. If possible, position the barbecue so that smoke doesn't waft into the house through open windows. Think also of the direction of the wind so that smoke doesn't drift into guests' eyes or neighbours' gardens while you are cooking.

Once you have sorted out the basics, decide on a theme for your barbecue party. Why not have a Country and Western style party where everyone wears checked

If your garden is a suitable size, you can build a permanent brick barbecue in a corner. Here, the green theme of the door and shutters is continued in the green checked table cloth, green plates, napkins and other accessories under a green sunshade.

Enamel plates, mugs and serving dishes provide the central focus for this cheerful picnic. Teamed with red and white checked napkins and a red table cloth, they combine durability with a sense of style.

shirts and denims, the table or tables are decorated with brightly coloured checked table cloths and napkins. This style of party doesn't really call for flower arrangements on the table, but if you want some sort of decoration, why not use colourful, empty beer or cola cans and arrange in them flowers that echo the colours in the labelling or a country theme. Before using a can like this, remove the top with a can-opener and ensure that the edges are smooth. An alternative to this table decoration is to use brilliantly coloured vegetables, such as green and red peppers and tomatoes, piled high on the table or in bowls.

Serve hamburgers and sausages and all the other traditional barbecue goodies. (Kebabs, although not traditionally Country and Western, are extremely popular at barbecues.) Serve drinks (cider, beer, punch, or

Far left: *Classic garden furniture and an eye-catching awning create the ideal setting for an informal drink in the sun. The simple addition of a vase of freshly-picked flowers makes all the difference.*

Left: *A picnic tea by the river is given an exotic flavour with the substitution of a decorative bedcover for the usual table cloth. Lemon tea served in oriental-style cups and carefully chosen serving dishes complete the setting.*

shandy), from large earthenware jugs. If the party takes place in the evening, light the garden with flares and candles or even have a small bonfire burning to set the atmosphere.

Teddy bears' picnic

To make a picnic that is memorable and fun have a teddy bears' picnic (down in the wood, if possible). Everyone should take along a favourite teddy bear and picnickers should wear some item of clothing that identifies them with a famous bear – a yellow and black checked scarf for Rupert or wellington boots and a luggage label for Paddington. The food should include typical bear favourites – honey and banana sandwiches, marmalade sandwiches, crunchy apple and coleslaw filling for pitta

Right: *A linen table cloth can be secured with tent pegs so it won't flap in the breeze during your picnic, such as this simple meal of bread, cheese and salad. Bring matching napkins, with a floral arrangement for an extra splash of colour.*

Far right: *Stunningly simple, this informal outdoor lunch uses colour with style. Team pink-checked napkins with complementary cutlery and keep food to a pink, green and cream colour theme, thrown into sharp focus by the use of glass plates and bowls.*

bread. Take disposable plates and mugs with bears on, if you can find any. If not buy plain white ones and stick or draw teddies on to the rim of the plates and the outside of the mugs. All the food should be manageable with fingers only – after all, no self-respecting bear would be seen eating with a knife and fork – it's always paws that get stuck into honey pots!

Decorate the rug or cloth where food is laid out with lots of tiny, toy teddies and sit all the guest teddies with them.

Other picnic ideas

Shipwreck picnic

For a shipwreck picnic, guests should be clad in tattered, ragged clothes and food should be slightly unusual to suggest having to live on whatever can be found on a desert island, or anything that was rescued or washed ashore. Here are some suggestions: prawns mixed with palm hearts in a little mayonnaise inside wholewheat pitta bread; fish in a lightly curried cream sauce made with coconut milk, mixed with cucumber or green pepper; fruit salad made with exotic fruits such as mangoes, lychees, pinapple, guavas in a brandy syrup.

Instead of plates find some thick strong leaves (you may want to do this before you set off from home so that

you know you've got them and that they have been washed!), or scallop shells. Eat with shells (such as mussel shells) and wrap paper mugs in more large leaves so that it looks as if the cups, too, are improvised.

'20s style picnic

For a sophisticated occasion have a '20s picnic in a stylish setting – by a lake or in the grounds of a stately home. Ask everyone to dress in appropriate style, with bow ties, boaters, and flimsy frocks and beads. Pack the food into wicker hampers and take cocktails ready mixed in thermos flasks or cocktail shakers packed in ice bags. Proper glasses, cutlery and china are called for, rather than disposable picnic ware. Take fruit garnishes ready to decorate the edge of the glasses. Lay rugs or blankets out on the ground and scatter cushions around for people to lounge against. If it's a really sunny day, take parasols or brightly coloured umbrellas to provide a little shade.

Family picnic

To make the food more interesting for children at a family picnic, pack their lunch or tea separately in individual boxes or their own lunch boxes, so that they can sit and delve into their own supply of goodies. Add an extra treat such as a chocolate mouse, a favourite candy bar, a baby cheese, or a packet of special nuts.

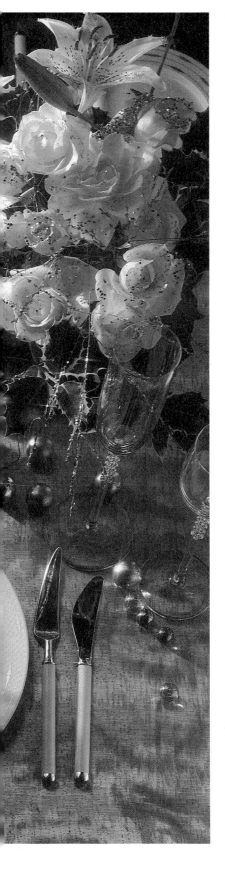

A SWELL NOEL

To organise a happy, successful and relaxed Christmas you need to start planning in October. If you leave everything until the last couple of weeks you will be absolutely worn out by Christmas Eve and you won't have the energy to enjoy yourself. Not only do you have the presents to worry about, there's the gift-wrapping to plan, the Christmas cake, the pudding and other traditional foods to make or order, the guest lists for various parties to draw up, the drink to order and all the decorations for house and table to plan, buy and arrange. If you start making lists in early November and spread the jobs and the shopping over six to seven weeks, you'll beat the crowds during the last minute rush, your head will spin a little less and you'll still have enough energy to enjoy all the festivities once they get going. You might even have enough energy to give a drinks party for friends you won't see on Christmas Day itself.

Christmas drinks party

For a Christmas drinks party arrange a table with a festive display of drinks and glasses. Swag the table with a rich red cloth (see page 73) and trim with bunches of holly or mistletoe or ivy. If the table is against the wall, place a cone arrangement of white, silver, red and green foliage and baubles in the centre at the back. To make this, first choose a base – a silver cakestand, or a wooden or chrome tray. Plate on it a cone of flower-arranging foam

A Christmas table should look festive and dramatic. Choose a colour scheme such as gold and silver, with elegant gold-patterned china, matching accessories, and seasonal floral decorations. A glamorous table setting such as the one shown here can be easily achieved with good advance planning.

about 2.5 cm (1 inch) smaller in diameter than the base itself. Wire all the glass baubles with firm pieces of wire. Arrange the first layer of white baubles interspersed with holly leaves. The second layer might be made up of poinsettia flower heads, silver baubles and sprigs of ivy, which should be positioned so that they rest above the first row. The third row is of white baubles again mixed in with ivy leaves and holly sprigs. Fill the top space with two poinsettia heads and sprigs of mistletoe or ivy.

Arrange the drinks around the centrepiece. You may like to serve punch from a large bowl. If so, decorate the handles of the bowl with curling ivy and mistletoe and perhaps curled gift-wrap ribbon in reds and greens. In spaces on the table arrange Christmas candleholders in the shape of Christmas trees or stars and burn red and silver candles. Red, wooden apples are available as candle holders, or use real apples with a hole cut for the taper or candle. Leave room on the table for trays of food to be placed, or set up a separate table for food. Serve appetising finger food and arrange it on trays that can be passed around easily.

If you use a round tray, place a decorative arrangement of mistletoe, or a miniature Christmas tree, or a bright Christmas bauble in the centre to add a touch of glamour to the food. Then organise the food in circles of various nibbles, working outwards from the decoration. If you use rectangular trays, arrange the food in alternate rows of different items. Leave a space in the middle for the decoration. If the trays are not going to be passed around amongst the guests, decorate the handles with swirls of twisted ribbons and ivy leaves. Other red and green garnishes add appeal to the trays of food – try small bunches of parsley, radish roses, spring onion curls, tomato baskets filled with cress or parsley, watercress, cocktail sticks of pieces of red pepper and twists of cucumber (see page 149 for ideas).

Meanwhile...

Christmas is a family time and children often accompany parents to celebrations. Although adults enjoy a drinks party children may find it very trying and get more and more bored. One way of avoiding this is to set up a children's party room to which they can escape and enjoy their own festivities while parents can continue theirs. If you have a regular babysitter or teenage relatives, ask them to supervise the proceedings and organise crackers and games and set up children's videos. The children

should have their own party food set out, if the room is large enough, as a picnic with a large paper cloth on the floor and disposable Christmas cups and plates. The Christmas cake could be a sponge and sugar paste Father Christmas, Christmas tree or snowman.

The Christmas table

There are many ways to create a festive table for your Christmas lunch or dinner. The decorative theme you choose can be dictated by the colour scheme of your

Christmas in the grand style! With such a magnificent dining table your setting should be in keeping and an extravagant table decoration doesn't look out of place. No table cloth is needed, and the fine white china and crystal glassware are the perfect accompaniments. The centrepiece is made by looping strings of silver and gold beads between tall gold candlesticks, with matching baubles, tinsel and gold ferns.

dining room, or the food and the china on which it is served. Ideas for non-traditional themes follow but to start with, here is a setting with a traditional Christmas theme.

Traditional Christmas

The colour theme is green and red, with an evergreen wreath decorated with silver bells and red ribbons at the front door and an abundance of greenery throughout the house. Poinsettias, with their flash of brilliant red flowers are ideal Christmas house plants and are made more festive by hanging delicate strands of silver tinsel over the leaf stems. Place clusters of holly, mistletoe and ivy in vases and round candlesticks.

Make a central decoration for the table by grouping tall, slender, red or silver candles with gently trailing, variegated ivy leaves and mistletoe or evergreen foliage. Cover the table with a white damask cloth and arrange the central decoration so that the tendrils of ivy and mistletoe lie gently on the cloth. Set the table and tie white linen napkins with either furled red ribbons or garlands of winter greenery, or roll into plain silver or bone napkin rings decorated with curling stems of ivy or mistletoe and bows of red, shiny ribbon.

Don't clutter the table with large crackers. Either buy tiny decorative ones or do without. Fill spaces on the table with silver or red and green dishes full of

Above: *The traditional colour theme of green and red is carried through in every detail, from candles on the table, glasses with green stems, and table decorations, to the Christmas tree, candelabra, evergreen wreath and unusual centrepiece of gourds and marrows.*

Right: *A white Christmas table looks elegant and stylish, especially when teamed with sparkling glassware, silver cutlery and dishes, and silver-painted fir cones among the floral decorations. Decorate the gifts with silver ribbon and white flowers.*

sweets wrapped in silver, gold or coloured foil, sugared almonds coated in bright green and red, silver and gold coated dragées and nuts. Before you start the meal, switch on the Christmas tree lights, light the candles and dim the electric lights and enjoy a really traditional Christmas meal.

A white Christmas

For an elegant and stylish Christmas table use as much white as possible with a touch of silver or gold and a bright splash of colour at each place setting in the form of a gift wrapped in stunning red, glittery paper. Cover the table with a white damask or lace cloth and fold matching napkins into one of the elaborate shapes on pages 141-2. Add a sprig of pale green foliage or a white flower to each napkin shape. For the centre of the table use a vase, which can be silver, white ceramic or crystal, filled with mixed white flowers and the very palest silvery-green foliage. Place tall, white tapers in slim, silver or glass

candlesticks. Set the table with pure white, plain china and elegant glasses. To give the table an extra gleam cut a few star shapes in different sizes from silver foil paper and lay these carefully on the cloth around the base of the candlesticks or vase, and a few near each place setting.

The final touch – the splash of colour – comes from the individual gifts at each place setting. Wrap the presents in the brightest red, shiny paper you can find and tie each with white pearlised or silver gift-wrap ribbon. Curl the ends to add a further festive touch and place the presents on each side plate or main plate. The overall effect will be quite stunning.

Blue and gold Christmas

If your dinner service is blue, or white and blue, it is as possible to create a Christmas table with blue as the dominant colour instead of red or green. As a tablecloth you could use a disposable paper cloth printed in soft marbled blues or a piece of blue satin or embossed, shiny blue fabric. A cheaper alternative is to cover the table in

Left: *If your dinner service has a blue pattern, a beautiful Christmas table can be created with a blue theme. Glass baubles placed in a bowl with candles make a glowing centre-piece.*

Above: *Yellow and red make a warm, glowing Christmas colour scheme. The shops will be full of little extras that you can incorporate into your table decorations to make your arrangement look really individual. Here, every available surface is covered with candles, lighting up the collection of festive decorations.*

shiny blue gift-wrap. Antique blue glasses edged with gilt would look wonderful but, if you don't own any, use your best glassware instead. At the centre of the table arrange white flowers in a blue vase or create a centre-piece with blue and white candles, gold ribbons and fresh white flowers or mixed blue and white silk flowers. Match napkins to the table cloth and tie with gold ribbon or tiny garlands of flowers to match the centrepiece. Buy blue and gold Christmas tree baubles in different sizes and place these in the gaps on the table. Curl blue, white and gold gift-wrap ribbon and lay gently around the glasses at each place setting. If you have gifts for each guest, wrap them in midnight blue shiny paper and decorate with a blue or gold gift tag.

Similar effects can be achieved with other colour schemes – green china with silver touches, pink china with silver and purple trimmings, black and white china with black, white and red or pink extras, or floral china with a cloth, candles and ribbons to match one of the predominant colours.

Ready-made Christmas touches

At Christmas the shops are full of little extras that you can incorporate into your table decorations. You will find mats in the shape of Christmas trees, snowmen, Father Christmases and paper table cloths and napkins printed with seasonal designs. Christmas tree baubles are easily adapted to make table decorations and some china manufacturers make plates decorated with Christmas trees and similar Christmas motifs. Choose with care and adapt with taste and your table will be really special.

PARTY TIME

Children's parties should be lively and colourful celebrations that mean lots of laughter for everyone and special treats for the birthday girl or boy or special guest. A party needs very careful planning and, unless it is a surprise event, should involve the child as much as possible, depending of course, on the age. It is fun to send hand-made invitations, giving the guests details, not only of where, when and why, but also whether they have to wear costume, or a funny hat, or bring something special. Choose a theme before you start, and plan the invitations, place cards, food, drink, games and fancy dress to match the chosen topic. The theme you choose will depend on the child's age, interests and tastes. Involve the child in deciding which food and drinks to serve and choose funny names for the different dishes to suit the theme. For instance, you might have a giggle trying to decide whether the fizzy drinks at a 'Monster' party should be called 'Giant Rat's Bath Water' or 'Frankenstein's Special Cocktail'. Organise a thematic novelty cake for the centre of the table.

Games and activities can also revolve around the main theme – name teams after main characters or name individual guests after different characters and adapt well-known games, such as 'Charades', 'Draw the Word' or 'Match the Face to the Name' to suit your particular topic.

A successful party should run smoothly. It is very important that young children are occupied all the time, so make sure that, as one activity finishes, the next one

begins. It's during the gaps that problems arise, so plan each game carefully, have ready all the props you need and, if possible, get other parents or adults to help run the proceedings. Organise the tea table well in advance – again with lots of help. Don't clutter the table with all the food at once. Set out savoury food first with just the novelty cake in the middle of the table, bring on the sweet things later. Decorate the table to suit the theme and use disposable napkins, plates and cups to save on the break-ages, spills and washing up. The kitchen or garden are ideal settings, but, if you have to use your dining or living room, cover the carpet with a dustsheet or blanket to protect it when food gets dropped or spilt.

A first birthday

For a first birthday party, the most important item is the cake in the middle of the table. Choose a suitable theme – for example, a teddy bear, or other favourite toy, and continue the theme across the table with tiny teddies in gaps between the plates of food, and napkins and table cloth repeating the motif, if you can find the right sort. Other ideas for a cake include a cake in the shape of a

Above: *Choose a theme, such as Father Christmas, for your children's party, and carry this through to every detail.*

Right: *Children's parties should be colourful, with disposable napkins, plates and cups to avoid breakages.*

number one, or a pile of building bricks made by covering cubes of sponge cake with coloured sugar paste. Write the number 1 on to several of the cubes with food colouring, and stack the cubes in a random and jolly arrangement.

Parties for three- to seven-year-olds

Ideal themes for this age group include colours; farmyard animals; toys (teddy bears or dolls); transport; favourite cartoon, storybook or TV characters; nursery rhymes; or any other theme that you think will particularly appeal to your guests!

A farmyard party

You may be able to find ideal invitation cards, tablecloths, plates, cups and paper hats printed with farmyard animals such as ducks, pigs and hens. If you can't, make your own invitations by cutting out white card in the shape of ducks, pink card in the shape of pigs, and draw in the details with felt-tipped pens. The table cloth can be either a plain cloth or a brightly printed one in the colours you want to use. You could decorate a plain white paper cloth yourself: draw on to it the outline of different animals and ask the children to colour them in at the party. If you can find animal napkin rings, roll the napkins into them. Alternatively, fold the napkins into triangles, place one on each child's plate and sit a sugar pig or chocolate hen on top. The birthday cake could be made in the shape of one of the animals or made as a round or square cake with sugar animals walking round the edge. Fill gaps on the table with farmyard toys – tractors, cows, horses and cockerels. Curl paper streamers around the cake and place a name card in the shape of one of the animals, at each child's plate.

A transport tea

Trains, cars, buses, planes, lorries, boats can all fit the theme – the scope is endless. Invitation cards could be cut in the shape of almost any vehicle, and the cake could be a brightly coloured version of one of the child's favourites. If you can't find a table cloth and napkins decorated with the right pictures, use a plain cloth with roads drawn on it in felt-tipped pen and dot toy cars, lorries or buses on it to set the scene. Fold napkins into the shape of little boats (see page 142) and, at each child's place, stand a name card in the shape of one of the vehicles. If you have the time, transform some plain cake boxes into

Right: An ideal theme for parties for three- to seven-year-olds would be transport, with suitable china, matching paper hats and small gifts. Make multi-coloured paper chains and strew sweets over the table to enhance the effect.

Inset: A castle is easy to make and provides a good theme for a young children's party. Use old cotton reels, straws and thick paper for the flags to go along the drawbridge.

miniature suitcases by clever use of felt-tip or paint, and let the children pretend that they are travelling on board the different vehicles. Their tea is packed inside the box with a bright napkin. A luggage label tied to each box also acts as a name card so that each guest knows where to sit.

Parties for eight- to 12-year-olds

Suitable themes for this age group are space, heroes and heroines, horses and ponies, sports (such as football, canoeing, snooker, motor racing), popular television characters (for example, favourite detectives or comedy acts) and pop singers.

A football tea

If the guests support a particular team they should come to the party wearing the colours of that team. The invitations could be shaped like a football, or a football shirt in the relevant colours. The cake could be a large football, or a football pitch: make a rectangular cake and cover with green icing and desiccated coconut, dyed with green food colouring, for the grass. Pipe lines in white icing and make the goal posts from lollipop sticks and a bit of fine netting. Position two teams of plastic players ready for the kick-off on the field. Lay the table with a cloth, napkins and china (or disposable table-ware) in the team's colours. Add some football paraphernalia to the table – a referee's whistle (if you can stand the noise) on a ribbon, a rosette, a rattle, a miniature football or two – and the scene is set.

A heroes and heroines party

Fancy dress is an absolute must for this party. The party and the table provide the setting for heroes and heroines from any era – the children decide on their costume. It is difficult to suit all the possible characters that may turn up, so choose a setting that is fairly neutral but special – a little in the style of the last scene of a traditional panto-mime – all white and gold and rather glamorous. Set the table with a disposable, gold-printed cloth or buy some gold netting and place it over a white undercloth. Use lots of gold and white streamers to decorate the table, to tie up napkins and to garland the cake in the middle. The cake could be a gold medal congratulating and rewarding 'Our Hero' or 'Our Heroine', followed by the birthday girl or boy's name. The cake can either be made with golden yellow sugar paste or covered carefully with gold foil paper which is removed before cutting. Place cards can be prepared before the party and filled in with the characters' names once you know who everybody is.

Parties for teenagers

Teenage parties need to be much more grown-up affairs. Here are a few ideas for suitable themes.

A Hammer House of Horror party

For teenagers, a horror theme always goes down well, so why not throw a Hammer House of Horror party? Send out invitations on black card shaped either like a skull marked with white bones, or shaped like a monster. Ask guests to come in costume. They could come as anything from Dracula with blood-covered fangs to the hunchback of Notre Dame.

Decorate the room with suitable horrors such as spooky skeletons made by painting white bones on black card, ghosts made by draping old white sheets over an upturned mop and with slits cut for the eyes and mouth, rubber spiders dangling on elastic from the ceiling. The room should be dark and eerie, so have concealed lighting with green or red bulbs or filters.

Cover the table with a black or grey cloth and place toy creepy-crawlies at strategic points, hanging over the edge and in the dishes of food; make spiders' webs with fine thread wound round white straws that have been fixed into a small ball of Plasticine. Hang ghastly masks in corners of the room or place in the middle of the table and paint them with red blood dripping from their mouths and eyes; buy rubber hands and feet from joke shops, paint them with warts and blood and stick tufts of fur or brown raffia on to look like hair. Place these ghoulish objects on the table and around the room to look as if they are sticking out of the walls and from the dishes of food. Give the food suitably unpleasant names – Monster's Blood Punch, Vampire Hot Pot, Witches Wedges (sandwiches or cakes), Chopped Lizard's Tongue cake.

Any party table will look good if you choose an exciting colour scheme and have lively decorations such as matching paper plates, napkins, straws, balloons and streamers.

A '60s party

A '60s theme for a teenage party is a good one as that period still symbolises the beginning of the pop music era, and more freedom for youngsters to let their hair

one corner to the edge of the table, and use old 45 rpm records bought from your local second-hand shop as plates and table mats. (Do make sure they are not rare and therefore worth a fortune!) The birthday or celebration cake could be made in the shape of a guitar, a record (made with black sugar paste and the record grooves marked on with a knitting needle), or even a model of the Beatles or other '60s group or star. Play the best music from the period and set up a name-the-group-or-singer competition.

Other themes suitable for teenagers are: a rock-and-roll party, a Hollywood party, a James Dean party, a Levis party, a spies party, and a science fiction party.

Halloween

This one is really fun. Send out invitations on cards in the shape of a witch on a broomstick, or a black cat. Ask people to come in costume.

Decorate the entire drinking and eating area with autumnal leaves, mock spiders, bats and other nasty-looking objects you can find in joke shops. You might even find a luminous skeleton! The room should be dark with candles burning inside pumpkins. Spread a black or dark coloured cloth over the table and decorate it with smaller pumpkins with candles burning inside, dried leaves, small rubber spiders and beetles and other creepy-crawlies. Even if it doesn't sound very appetising, your party should be great fun and have guests shrieking with laughter rather than horror.

A party on pancake day

You need to decide whether you want to serve savoury or sweet pancakes, as two courses might leave guests incapable of moving!

If you decide on a savoury course, plan a very light starter and dessert. If you decide on a pancake pudding, serve a light main course so that guests can enjoy tucking in afterwards. If you have enough room in the kitchen hold the party there so that each guest can cook his or her own pancake.

The table should be set for an informal supper or lunch. As this event takes place in the spring, choose light spring colours: put a pot of crocuses or a vase of daffodils or narcissi in the centre of the table, or fill a fruit bowl with apples, bananas, lemons, limes and oranges. Use paper napkins in two colours to tone with your scheme, for example, yellow and white. Unfold the napkins and

down and have some fun. Invitation cards could be in the shape of a record.

Move furniture out of the way to make room for dancing, and put up posters of the pop and rock idols of those days around the room. Add a few streamers and balloons to brighten up the walls. Set up a buffet table at one side of the room with drinks and food spread out ready. To decorate the table, pin old record sleeves by

For a party on pancake day choose light spring colours for the plates and napkins and decorate the table with matching spring flowers such as tulips, daffodils and freesias.

lay a yellow one on top of a white, to form an eight-pointed star. Pick both napkins up together pinching the middle firmly and loosely shaping them into a cone. Place the tip of each cone inside a glass, mug or cup, and arrange the napkins so that both colours show.

When you are ready for the pancake course, bring to the table one large dish or several smaller dishes containing the fillings and sauces so that everyone can help themselves. For savoury pancakes serve a mixture of chicken, mushrooms, green peppers or leeks; shrimps and white fish; bacon, spinach and tomatoes; or tuna fish and cheese. Fill a sauce boat or bowl with a creamy

poached with a little sugar or honey. Also place ready on the table a pot of maple syrup and a pot of jam. Help the children to cook and toss their own pancakes and then to fill them with the different mixtures.

Bonfire night

A firework party can be a tea party that takes place before setting off fireworks at home or going to an organised display, or it can be a buffet or sit-down supper that follows the evening's entertainment.

At a tea party for young children the table could be set with a bright flame-coloured cloth. Crepe paper is ideal. Cut strips of different coloured paper – shades of orange, yellow and red – and lay them so that they overlap and cover the table. A Guy Fawkes cake makes the best centrepiece. One way to make such a cake is to cook a sponge mixture in an oven-proof pudding basin. When cool, turn it upside down, cover it with butter icing in flame colours and press broken chocolate flake into the icing to look like burning firewood. On the top sit a guy made from sugar paste or marzipan, painted with food colourings to create a face and details of clothing. An alternative method is to crumple flame-coloured tissue or crepe paper on to a tray or plate. Arrange chocolate finger biscuits as the logs of the bonfire and place a guy modelled from sugar paste or marzipan on top.

Set the children's places with china, or disposable party-ware that matches the bright, flame colours, and add napkins to match. In amongst the dishes of savouries and cakes set little clusters of indoor fireworks and a glass full of sparklers. Burn candles during the meal and, once all the food has been devoured, enjoy the fireworks under strict supervision, of course.

For a buffet or sit-down meal after the firework display is over, set the table with a cloth and crockery in warm colours and have candles burning ready for when your guests come in from the cold. Make the room look really inviting with an open fire glowing in the hearth and the candles burning around the room as well as on the table. Serve baked potatoes with cream cheese or butter, or cheddar and crispy bacon fillings; thick carrot and parsnip or creamy vegetable soup; sausages; hamburgers and meat pies. Decorate the table with indoor fireworks and scatter flame-coloured streamers in spaces on the table. As a centrepiece, group several candles together on a mirror or shiny tray to cast a warm, flickering light over the meal table.

or cheesy sauce to pour over the filled pancakes.

For sweet pancakes arrange a plateful of quarters of orange, lemon and lime, ready for squeezing over the freshly-tossed pancakes, or dishes of stewed apple with raisins and nutmeg or cinnamon, crushed bananas with lemon juice and brown sugar, or any soft fruit lightly

FLOWERS AND FANTASIES

Flowers make traditional and beautiful table decorations but other things can be used. When choosing the materials for a table decoration, bear in mind the type of occasion for which the arrangement will be used, the food that you are going to serve, the china to be used, the colour scheme, the size of arrangement that you need and, if appropriate, the decorative theme. For example, the table at a fifth wedding anniversary for which the symbol is wood, could be attractively decorated with an arrangement including unusual pieces of bark or wood enhanced with berries or foliage; a table for a meal of seafood might be decorated with shells and plants that echo the sea and beach; willow pattern china might inspire a decoration of willow branches and catkins; an Art Nouveau table setting demands lilies and other rather exotic and curvaceous flowers and leaves.

How to choose flowers and foliage

Choose at least two different shapes of flowers or leaves for your decoration to provide natural variety or contrast. Spiky flowers such as stocks, irises and freesias go well with more rounded roses, dahlias, carnations or daffodils. Tapering foliage harmonises with more bushy branches. Remember that unusual items will be noticed more readily and possibly provoke conversation – rosehips are more unusual than roses, hosta flowers are seen less frequently in arrangements than their leaves. Be aware of any overpowering scents that may be rather too strong for mealtimes.

The colours you choose should tone with the decor of the room and the china and linens used. It is not always necessary to pick out the obvious, main colour in a patterned china. Instead, select a secondary or very minor colour and choose flowers accordingly. Your arrangement should involve more than one colour as a single colour can look flat and lack interest. There should, however, be a main colour accented, rather than equalled, by a secondary balancing colour.

Above: *An unusual table decoration created with shells in the shape of a flower.*

Left: *Flowers make beautiful table decorations. Because the room and dining table are large, they can carry this extravagant-sized arrangement of summer garden flowers, spread the length of the table using several vases.*

The care of picked flowers

Flowers and foliage that have been carefully arranged can droop and wither far more quickly than expected. This can of course be due to the lack of care they received before you bought them, but it may be due to lack of correct care after you have brought them home. With the right treatment flowers can last longer.

First, strip off all the leaves that will be below the water line, re-cut the stems and then put them into clean water as soon as possible and leave in a cool place to have a long drink. Flowers that are at all wilted should

be put into warm water. Stems should be cut diagonally across so that they don't rest flat on the bottom of the vase so cutting off the water supply.

Different stems need different treatments. Hard and woody stems should have 2.5 cm (1 inch) at the bottom of the stem stripped of bark, then be split or gently hammered. Soft stems such as lilies and narcissi should be cut at an angle and placed immediately in water. Plants which exude sap should stand in water for an hour or so on their own to give the sap a chance to drain away. Hollow stems such as dahlias and hollyhocks should be cut, turned upside down and the stems filled with warm water and plugged with cottonwool. Any stems which 'bleed' such as poppies and dandelions should have the tip of the stem singed briefly in a candle flame.

To prolong the life of cut flowers and foliage, and to keep the water clean and bacteria free, try the following:
● A copper coin in the bottom of the vase.
● An aspirin dissolved in the water.
● Two teaspoonsful of sugar or half a teaspoonful of honey to a pint of water.
● Brand-name, commercially-produced long-life crystals.

Containers

Choose a vase for each occasion very carefully. It doesn't have to be a traditional, purpose-made vase: anything that is, or can be made watertight, will make a good vase – a large shell, a wooden jewellery box (with water-tight container inside), a china jug, a cup, a tea pot, a pewter tankard, a tray or pretty plate. Let your imagination run free in order to find a container that will suit the theme of a particular meal and a particular blend of flowers or fruits.

If you need to use smaller, less attractive containers inside the decorative one make sure that they are well hidden.

Essential equipment

In order to create successful centrepieces for the table you need patience, a willingness to experiment and a few basic pieces of equipment:
● Two or three metal pinholders with solid, heavy bottoms and sharp prongs of varying thicknesses for holding different types of stems.
● Wire netting with a 3-5 cm (1½-2 inch) mesh so that the wire can be squeezed and shaped and pushed into differently shaped containers.
● Water-retaining plastic foam that holds flowers in position. It can be cut to suit any container and can be used in conjunction with pinholders and wire to allow maximum holding power for stems of different thicknesses.
● Reel wire and stub wires – it is sometimes necessary to wire stems in order to straighten or strengthen them, and therefore to have more control over their shape and direction. The wire can be bought at floral art suppliers or garden centres.
● Florists' tape – a green adhesive tape which is essen-

tial when wiring or strengthening stems.
● Cocktail sticks to hold berries and fruit in place.
● Secateurs and scissors for splitting stems and trimming off leaves and rose thorns.

The principles of flower arranging

The shape and effect that you create does not have to conform to any hard and fast rules – you should follow your instinct, let simplicity and naturalness rule, and create something beautiful or striking to suit yourself and the occasion.

Decide first on the position the arrangement is to occupy – the centre of a dining table, the centre back of a buffet table, the corner of an occasional table or a tray. The position will affect the shape and symmetry, depending on whether it will be seen from all sides and above, as in the middle of a dining table, or from only three sides, as on a buffet table against a wall.

The size of the arrangement will depend on the space available and the height should be such that it doesn't obstruct people's view of each other across the table. A centrepiece should be a low arrangement, approximately 30 cm (1 foot) or less high, or should be on a raised pedestal or in a tall, narrow vase that is over 60 cm (2 feet) tall. The raised arrangement can include trailing flowers and foliage, but these should not intrude on the space across which guests are trying to communicate. You may choose to arrange the flowers to echo the shape of the table – a round display for a round table, a long and narrow grouping for a rectangular or oval table. Depending on the number of places and the space available, the flowers don't necessarily have to be in the middle, they could equally well be at one end or along one side of the table.

Traditional shapes

Traditional arrangements are those which have the overall shape of a circle, a triangle, an oval or a diamond. These all demand a degree of symmetry, and are based on the principle that all the stems radiate outwards from a central stem. It is important to fix this central stem first, using a straight, fairly tall flower or branch. Around this axis arrange the other stems, all leaning away – to a lesser degree when nearly as tall as the central piece and close to it, and to a greater degree if shorter and further away. Always work on the whole arrangement, distributing the flowers and foliage evenly and trying to

balance them. Don't try to complete one small area before moving to the next. Use flowers at different stages of opening, some with buds fully open and some quite tightly closed, and mix the colours carefully.

It is a good idea to work on the arrangement in the lighting in which it will eventually be seen, as different lighting can ruin the effect and cast shadows where you hadn't expected. Overhead lighting will give a certain brilliance to the flowers and cast the lower ones into the shade; side lighting may cast half the arrangement into the shade.

Modern and abstract designs

Depending on your decor you may want to improvise and experiment with sparser, more dramatic arrange-

Let simplicity and naturalness be the key in floral arrangements. Sparse, dramatic Ikebana-like designs suit ultra-modern or minimalist interiors, especially if your dining room is decorated in the Japanese style or if you are going to serve a Japanese meal.

ments that suit ultramodern or minimalist interiors. A piece of twisted cane set into a wooden base with seed heads wired at intervals on the curves; a few tall, sword-like leaves from such a plant as 'Mother-in-Law's Tongue' arranged in a stark ceramic dish with one or two flower heads; one dramatic brilliantly-coloured flower, such as a 'Bird of Paradise' or an amaryllis, arranged in a tall jug with one or two ferns or hosta leaves. Whatever you use and however you arrange it, make sure it is in proportion to the table or tray it is decorating.

Above: *For a spring arrangement use white flowers such as freesias, cow parsley, May blossom and white roses.*

Above right: *The bright colours of summer can be reflected in an arrangement that is yellow, orange, pink and red.*

Seasonal flower arrangement

It is obviously sensible to use seasonal flowers. Explore your area for the best florist, as the quality and variety of what they sell can vary. If no cultivated flowers suit your chosen theme, see what the countryside can offer, but be careful not to pick protected species.

Spring

Here are some ideas for table arrangements using spring flowers:

Using a metal ring mould filled with plastic foam, use anemones in purples, reds and streaked white to create a ring of colour. Shorten the stems to within 3-5 cm (1½-2 inches) of the head and push carefully into the soaked foam. Push sprigs of fern between the flower heads.

Fill a row of tall, glass storage jars or plain glass vases with pink water, made by using a few drops of deep pink food colouring and stand one or two tall, pink tulips in each vase. Add one tall leaf from the tulips and arrange the jars in a line down the middle of the table.

Deep blue jars or vases look wonderful with bright yellow daffodils. Divide daffodils and a few sprigs of mimosa

with one or two leaves between one or more vases and group the vases together in the middle of the table. If you don't have blue jars, use plain glass vases and colour the water blue with a few drops of food colouring.

Bulbs grown in pots also make stylish table decorations. Single hyacinths at each place setting or in a row down the centre of the table are particularly effective. Bowls of tightly-packed, flowering spring bulbs can also be used, especially if planted in a decorative bowl.

Summer

In early summer it's sometimes difficult to find enough flowers to make an attractive table decoration without paying a lot of money. Irises are at their best in June and are excellent flowers for sparse arrangements in tall, narrow vases. In July, the first of the sweet peas are ready for picking. As they are such delicate flowers, either float a mass of flower heads in a clear glass bowl or on a tray, or arrange them with a little greenery in an attractive teapot or a glass jug. For individual arrangements at each place setting arrange a few heads in egg cups, rice bowls or wine glasses.

Use pink dianthus and early pale pink roses to create a pink arrangement. Add some of the greeny-grey leaves from the dianthus and one or two taller leaves from garden shrubs. Arrange them in a silver rose bowl or fruit bowl, fixing them firmly into wire and plastic foam.

Wild flowers can make a very attractive arrangement, but the flowers often don't last very long. Many species

Above left: *For autumn, arrange golden oranges in a glass bowl. Cut off their peel in swirling patterns.*

Above: *In winter, use gourds, honesty and other dried flowers and grasses in suitable colours to decorate the table.*

are protected and you should be extremely wary of picking any wild flowers. Grasses and ferns can make eye-catching decorations either arranged together in a container or as individual specimens set in single containers around the table so that they resemble a small jungle. Ensure that they are tall so that diners can talk beneath and between them. Hedgerow foliage can be used in arrangements with garden flowers. The loose effect of the wild foliage sets off cultivated flowers rather well.

Autumn

In the autumn, wild berries and fruits, mixed with foliage that has turned from green to golden brown, make very effective displays. Choose a container that reflects the amber shades – copper, or china decorated with rich golds and yellows – and arrange stems of copper beech, red teasels, golden ears of wheat and a few white daisy chrysanthemums or ox-eye daisies.

Almost anything from the vegetable garden, fruit bowl or hedgerow can be transformed into a spectacular table arrangement – blackcurrants hanging gently from their stem mixed with autumn leaves and grasses, tangerines mingling with flaming orange chinese lanterns and dried cow parsley.

Most fruits and flowers are happy together, but ripe apples can give off a gas which makes some flowers close up. To keep vegetables and fruits in place, use small holders such as egg cups, cream cartons, napkin rings or blocks of indented plastic foam concealed beneath

each item, and use cocktail sticks to spear the different things together. Berries, currants and grapes are best wired first to a strong stem.

For a minimalist effect on an autumn table use an unusual piece of bark and fix a cube of plastic foam into the middle. Push a stem of tall pampas grass into it, just off-centre. Next to it, and just in front, fix a tall stem of love-in-the-mist seed heads that have been sprayed gold. At the base of the arrangement fix the head of one golden chrysanthemum with its head just above the bark. The display will have a very Japanese look and gives an effective decoration using a small number of flowers.

Winter

In winter, when there is little in the garden and flowers from the florist are expensive, use dried flowers or wild grasses to decorate the table. Bare twigs can be used in Japanese ikebana-style arrangements, and teasels and bulrushes are large enough to give interest to a vase of tall grasses. For the table, create either very tall decorations with tall, narrow vases filled with pampas grass so that it is above the line of vision, or arrange shorter stems in a small basket so that the overall shape spreads outwards rather than upwards. Glossy gift-wrap bags in gold and silver or dark green make ideal containers for small dried flower arrangements. Weight the bags with Plasticine or flat stones, place a piece of plastic foam into each bag and then push the stems of grasses and dried flowers into it, varying the height of the flowers so that they are not symmetrical, but emerge from the bags in a fairly random, loose way.

Dried flowers are ideal in cottage settings or set against stripped pine. They need displaying rather delicately, as a container that is too big or hefty will detract from the whispy quality of the flowers. Ideal containers are baskets, porcelain vases or bowls, or shells. They can also be arranged under a glass dome. For a covered display under a glass cheese dome or Victorian dome, choose dried hydrangea heads, orange statice, yellow heads of yarrow and silvery honesty leaves. Fix them firmly into the base to form a rounded shape. When the overall effect has been achieved add a few sprigs of tiny dried rosebuds.

Candles and flowers

When a low arrangement is needed for a table, candles are ideal for providing vertical interest and variety of line. They should enhance the colour scheme and their shape and height should suit the flowers. Candles should be introduced to an arrangement at the stage when the central stem has been put in place and you have decided the basic shape and dimensions.

Slim tapers can be pushed into plastic foam which will hold them steady. Heavier, taller candles need more support. Use either specially made plastic or metal candle holders (available from floral art suppliers) which push easily into plastic foam, or tape cocktail sticks, or pieces of stub wire to the lower end of the candle.

Fantasies

Don't feel that you always have to use flowers on the table. There are plenty of alternatives for occasions when you can't get any flowers, or when you would like a change. Here are some ideas:

- Scatter or arrange different types of shells across the middle of the table, or around each place setting.
- Glass baubles of the sort that are made for Christmas trees look wonderful in a large glass bowl, or scattered across the table. Use colours to suit the overall theme.
- Pebbles, rocks, pieces of driftwood or even pieces of coal can be very effective; group pebbles together on a tray or in a bowl; use wood or coal to create Japanese -style arrangements.
- Feathers and feathered creatures – replica birds and butterflies to empty spaces on the table cloth. Place a a table decoration. Trim a swagged cloth with white, papier-mâché and feather doves, or fix feather-winged butterflies to empty spaces on the tablecloth. Place a bunch of coloured feathers in a simple vase for the middle of the table. Peacock feathers create an oriental feel.
- A vase of silk flowers is often as attractive as the real thing, since today's silk flowers are deceptively real and are often made in unusual, exotic colours that blend well with more unusual colour schemes. Use silks to decorate the centre of the table or to add colour to each individual place setting by winding them around napkins, twining them around the stems of wine glasses or placed in individual, small vases.
- For a 'high tech' table setting, use a selection of shiny chrome tools – nuts, bolts and screws. Scatter them at random across the table, tumble them out of glass containers, or use them as knife rests. They look particularly good on glass, perspex, chrome or metal tables.
- Plain or coloured marbles in a glass or china bowl add sparkle to the table, particularly if burning candles are placed nearby and are reflected by the glass.
- Origami (folded paper sculptures) can provide interesting and unusual shapes to decorate individual areas of the table, or as part of a larger decoration. Cut a small, bare branch from a twiggy tree. Hang origami shapes from its twigs with black cotton. The branch can be laid in the centre of the table or propped in a shallow dish (use stones) to represent a small tree.
- Miniature gardens can be created with interesting stones, twigs, flowers and mosses. Try to use different textures, colours and shapes to reflect the variety of a real garden and to create a miniature landscape. A long rectangular garden could be made to run along the middle of the table, or use a round tray for a round or oval table.
- Grasses of different textures and colours can decorate the table by simply being laid across the middle, or at each place. They also look effective in a vase or bowl, or in a series of slim vases grouped together, or standing in a row.
- Make a miniature tree from a twiggy branch and hang interesting and appropriate objects from the branches

Left: *Shells scattered across the table make an interesting display, especially if there is fish or sea food on the menu. They look best against a plain background in a toning colour.*

Below: *Candles are ideal for providing vertical interest in a floral arrangement. They should enhance the colour scheme and their height and shape should suit the flowers.*

– foil covered chocolate pennies, Easter eggs, tiny gifts, feathered creatures etc. Fix the twig firmly into plastic foam in a vase or bowl sturdy enough to make a steady base.

Try combining some of these different effects, placing some in the middle of the table and others at place settings – a twig tree in the middle could be decorated with butterflies and one bird, and a bird could be placed at each setting to echo the theme. Fill a large glass bowl with silvery baubles for the middle and place two or three of different sizes and colours with a silk flower at each setting. Combine a few pebbles with grasses and twigs to make a Japanese ikebana arrangement and at each setting place an origami paper shape. Mix and match to find effects that suit your table and style.

Ribbons, garlands and streamers

Ribbons and streamers can be used to add a very festive touch to an otherwise ordinary table setting. It's a little like the difference made to a gift package by adding a ribbon, a bow and curled streamers. The final touch of swirling ribbons on a table makes it special.

Ribbons need to be matched in colour and width

to the colour and scale of the table setting. For example, a setting for two on a small table demands narrow streamers and small bows, whereas a wedding buffet table, for 150 guests, requires 10-12 cm (4-5 inch) wide ribbons and large swags and bows. Use satin ribbons or shiny gift-wrap ribbon, which has the advantage of holding the curl that you put into it by rubbing the edge of a knife or scissors down one side of the ribbon. Try some of the following ideas.

- Insert a piece of dowel in the centre of a flower arrangement, having first painted or sprayed the wood to tone with the arrangement. Attach long streamers to the top of the dowel, curl and twist them, then drape them so that they lie loosely across the table cloth. Very long streamers can hang between the place settings, reaching right down to the hem of the table cloth.
- Tie napkins with velvet, satin or gift-wrap ribbon and finish with a bow leaving the ends trailing on to the side plate or table cloth.
- Arrange a trail of curling ribbons or paper streamers around the central decoration or round each guest's place setting. Streamers also look very pretty twisting gently around the stems of wine glasses.
- Thread narrow satin ribbon through a lacy paper doyley and use to decorate cake plates or side plates.
- Decorate the edge of a buffet table with swags and bows made by twisting and looping wide, shiny ribbon. Fix it in place with drawing pins, stitches or adhesive tape.

Table cloths

The table cloth is extremely important, as it is the background for the table setting, the flowers and the food. Choose the fabric according to the occasion: fairly coarse linen is suitable for everyday meals; a starched damask is wonderful for formal dinners; a shiny satin gives a luxurious, extravagant air and helps reflect light from candles and lamps; a white lace cloth creates a rather delicate feminine background; and a layer of tulle or net sets a theatrical, flamboyant mood.

For a country house effect, spread a plain undercloth that hangs almost to the floor, then lay another, patterned cloth over the top. Gather the edges of the top cloth into deep swags and secure with bows (see page 73). A circular cloth with inset gussets of contrasting coloured fabric can add a new dimension to the colour scheme.

Different levels on which to display food at a buffet can be created by placing sturdy boxes in different sizes on the table top. Drape a richly textured cloth over boxes and table. If using satin or net on a dinner table, gather it slightly all over so that gentle folds and ripples of fabric lie between the plates and dishes. It gives the table richness and depth and creates a mood of indulgence and luxury.

If you don't have a supply of fine linen or cotton cloths, don't worry. There are other table covers that can look just as attractive and effective for particular occasions. Don't be afraid to improvise using a bedspread, sheet, curtain, shawl or paper.

Strips of crepe paper can be laid across or down

Far left, above: *Use ribbons and streamers to add a festive touch to a floral arrangement, choosing the colour and width of the ribbon to go with the table setting. Here, light purple ribbon is tied round a vase of purple pansies, matching the flowers on the china's design.*

Far left, below: *Table cloths provide an important background for the table setting. This richly textured gold cloth gives a luxurious, extravagant air for a formal dinner, and harmonises with the unusual wallpaper, gold chairs and gold-rimmed china. No centrepiece is required on such a beautiful cloth, with only simple floral arrangements.*

Left: *A white, lace-edged table cloth creates a delicate feminine atmosphere, and the rich pink undercloth matches the unusual table decoration of cloth flowers and leaves.*

the table. Crimp the edges first by gently stretching the sides. Mix different colours for special themes – red, white and blue for a British or French party, yellow and blue for a desert island dinner, red and green for an Italian pasta party.

Paint lining paper with bright colours or colour washes to create particular colour combinations – for a midsummer party in the garden, use blues, yellows and tinges of violet; for a Halloween buffet, paint the paper black and grey with yellow stars and magic symbols. Try crumpling the paper before laying it over the table. To hold it in place, use drawing pins if the table under-

neath is an old one. Alternatively, lay an old blanket on a good table and pin the paper to that.

Silver foil is an excellent substitute for a cloth and also adds a festive touch. Use it to cover the entire table, or as an undercloth over which to lay lace or swagged satin or linen, or lay a strip down the middle or diagonally across the table.

Glossy, gift-wrap paper adds colour and shine to a table. Join strips together with adhesive tape before laying over the table. Try using a mixture of colours for particular colour themes, or laying the paper underneath a lace or open-weave cloth.

ILLUMINATING IDEAS

When planning the lighting for a dining room or a part of the house which is used as a dining area, it is important to remember that the room in which you eat may be used for other functions as well. In a family house children may do their homework at the dining table, the worktop in a kitchen may have to double as a cooking surface and a breakfast bar. The lighting in the dining area may have to adapt to suit family meals, dinner parties, breakfasts and romantic dinners for two. Natural light may vary from brilliant sunlight streaming in one minute to the grey, dingy light of a thunder and rain storm the next. Even in the middle of the day, you may need to have some electric lighting. Plan your range of lights carefully so that each room in which you eat can be used in these different situations.

You should also notice the effects created by different sorts of lighting. Be aware, first, of natural light entering the room. Too much glare from the sun may make people around the table uncomfortable as they have to squint into direct rays of light. If so, fit blinds that can be lowered to suit the conditions. If the blinds are in use you may need other peripheral lighting in the room, on a high shelf or side table to counteract the loss of natural light.

This dining area adjoins the sitting room, so the style of lighting has been chosen to blend harmoniously. Blinds in the dining room cut out any glare from the sun which might make diners uncomfortable, and adequate lighting counteracts the loss of natural light.

When considering artificial light there are many options. A central pendant light hung above casts a pool of light that focuses attention on the table and shuts out other areas of the room, creating a feeling of intimacy, and drawing the diners together in a warm atmosphere conducive to conversation. Be careful, however, with pendants as they can cause a glare into guests' eyes. The most useful sort are those that can be moved up and down to suit the occasion. A rise and fall system with a dimmer switch will give a great deal of versatility to suit family occasions, daytime meals, evening dinner parties and informal suppers.

If you want to create an illusion of space in a small dining area, arrange the lights so that there are several around the perimeter of the room – on side tables, recessed lighting in cornices, wall lights casting light upwards on to walls and ceiling, floor lights that can be directed at walls and plants, strip lighting above pictures and wall hangings that give light to a particular focal point without the bulb being directly visible. This sort of side lighting will give a gentle glow to a room. Extra lighting on the table can be provided by candles both on the table and around the room. The flickering light cast by candles adds romance and intimacy, and is suitable in any situation.

Candles are generally better than table lights for adding extra, direct light on the table itself. However, in some situations small table lamps are effective. If two or three people are dining around a square or round table a lamp can be placed on the unused side. This has a similar effect to a pendant, bathing the table in a private supply of light and therefore drawing guests together. This sort of lamp on a busier, fuller table takes up too much room, and can block vision, thus impeding communication rather than helping it. If you do want to place lamps on the table, use very low ones and do be very careful about the position of trailing flexes.

Candles

Try placing candles in different positions on the table for different effects. Here are a few ideas:
- Using small candle holders to fit the overall theme, place a candle at each setting.
- Group several small, low candles together on a shiny tray, mirror or tray covered with silver foil. The flames and the light will be reflected so that the table is bathed in intensified, flickering light.

- Group several candles of varying colours or all the same colour to fit a particular theme, and to match the table linens, china and flowers. Choose the holders carefully so that they too, fit the colour scheme.
- Arrange candles down or across the middle of the table. If you don't have matching holders use small glasses, small bread rolls of interesting shapes or fruits that stand firm enough to hold the candle steady – for example apples, oranges, limes or lemons.
- Float special floating candles in bowls or trays of water. Colour the water with food colouring so that the tinted water and candles tone with the overall colour theme. Mix floating candles with floating flower heads but be careful the petals don't catch alight.
- Create steps of light by placing candles at different levels. In the centre of the table, position building blocks wrapped in silver or gold foil to form steps. Place the candles in holders on the different blocks.
- Choose different styles and sizes of candles for different occasions. Large, chunky candles are good for informal occasions where pottery is being used. Finer

Above: *These special candles are floated in a bowl of water, with mistletoe included for a romantic touch.*

Right: *A warm yellow glow is created with these candles, which also highlight the fine collection of glassware displayed on glass shelves. The candles are set in a glass bowl and on small, frosted glass plates to increase their radiance.*

tapers and slim candles are better for formal dinners. Children love shaped candles, and candles with a theme are effective as part of a thematic decoration.

● For an outdoor dinner, lanterns are fun and can be stood on the table or hung from a wall. Choose lanterns with plain glass for a clear light or coloured glass to cast coloured light over the table. Lanterns may also be suitable for indoor occasions, for example when the theme is rustic, or for Halloween.

Fairy lights

To add an unusual dimension to your table try stringing fairy lights across the table instead of using more conventional forms of lighting. Trail the flex carefully down the middle, wind the lights round vases and other ornaments, or curl the entire flex into a glass container so that the light is contained in a small area. Fairy lights can also be woven into a decoration involving fruit and flowers. Do be careful with the flex and tape it to the underside of the table so that people don't trip over it. Although the lights should be safe on cloths and paper, check every now and again that they are not overheating.

Torches

Torches can be very effective as part of a table decoration or as individual ornaments in themselves, to give sharp rays of light across the table. To form part of a decoration push the bases of three or four slimline torches into plastic foam so that the beams of light are directed upwards. Arrange flowers, feathers, silk flowers or foliage around them so that the heads of the torches are concealed but the light shines from their midst. For a high tech setting position several torches so that their beams criss-cross on the table top. This could be a good effect for Halloween or horror parties where light should be kept to a minimum.

Far left: *Fairy lights strung on decorative branches make an attractive change from the traditionally-lit Christmas tree in this simple, uncluttered dining room. The candles, lamp, soft overhead light and fire provide extra brightness.*

Left: *Different sources of light give different colours, so choose your dining room colour scheme carefully according to what type of lighting you will be using.*

Lighting and colour

Different sources of light give different colours. An everyday tungsten light bulb gives a yellowish light that enhances oranges and reds but deadens blues and purples. Candlelight also gives a yellowish light but dimmer than electric lighting. It is therefore flattering to skin tones but less kind to blues, purples and darker shades. Fluorescent lighting which is only really suitable in commercial or industrial areas, or possibly in work-rooms and garages at home, enhances blues and purples but kills reds and neutralises yellows. It is important to remember this if arranging flowers under strip lighting or when choosing fabrics or wall paints.

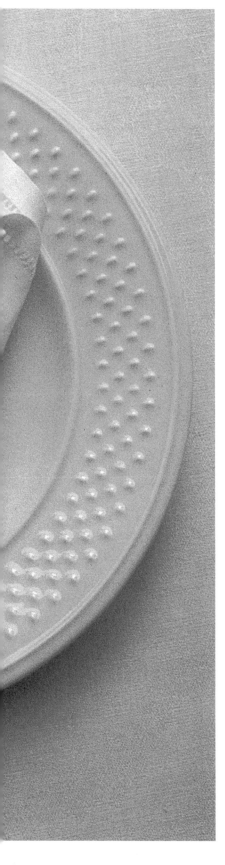

PRETTY PRACTICAL

The ideas in this book have, so far, been inspirational. In this chapter you will find practical instructions for making everything from a Christmas cracker to a radish rose.

Caring for tableware

Linens

Cotton and linen table cloths, napkins and place mats can be machine washed. Embroidered lace or lace trimmed items are best washed inside a pillow case in the machine to stop the delicate pieces being too harshly tossed around. If white fabrics become a little grey with age, add a small amount of gentle bleach or a blueing agent to the rinsing water. Boiling whites every now and then will also help to retain their whiteness. All natural fibres can be starched except fabrics which have a puckered finish, such as cotton seersucker.

After ironing linens, especially when using starch, fold the cloths carefully so that diamond-shaped creases don't appear when you open out the cloth to use it.

When ironing damp linens, iron from the centre out and gently pull the cloth or napkin into shape.

Glassware

A dishwashing machine should not be used to wash fine crystal or other valuable glasses. They should be washed in clean, fairly hot, soapy water and rinsed in clean

Crisp white linen can enhance your table setting and is very versatile. For seasonal themes embellish napkins with different coloured ribbons, flowers or small gifts. This yellow ribbon, mimosa and Easter Egg, on a yellow plate and table cloth, would suit an Easter table.

warm water. To prevent chipping the bases or edges, wash one glass at a time and drain on tea-towels or kitchen paper. Glasses should be dried and polished while still warm.

Engraved or cut glass may need a gentle scrub with a soft brush to remove any grease or dust. To remove any stains that won't come off in the wash, leave to soak in a solution of detergent for 24 hours, then wash normally, rubbing carefully at the marked spot.

If glass stoppers become wedged in the neck of decanters or storage jars, rub a little cooking oil around the join and stand in a warm place for 24 hours or so – the two parts should eventually slide apart.

China

Water that is too hot and strong, or undiluted washing-up liquids, can in the long term, damage the colour and glaze on fine china. Porcelain and bone china should be washed in clean, soapy water, and then rinsed, drained, dried and polished. They can be washed in a dishwashing machine as long as there is no gold-leaf or other precious metal finish to them. Never use a harsh scouring agent or abrasive on china as the glaze will be easily damaged.

Keep coloured and decorated china away from direct sunlight as the colours will fade and spoil. When storing bone china, give it plenty of room and don't stack plates and saucers without a layer of tissue or soft cloth between each to stop scratching and chipping. It is best not to hang fine china cups from their handles as they are quite delicate – stand them upside down, each on a saucer.

Cutlery

Don't leave cutlery lying around covered in food, grease or water. It's much better to wash it straight away before food can stain it. Salt is particularly risky as, in combination with hot water, it can cause pitting. Always wash and dry everything immediately after a meal. Wash each piece in clean, warm, soapy water, rinse and dry.

Don't leave bone-handled knives in water as the cement will soon weaken and loosen, and the handles will come away from the blades. Don't throw cutlery into the washing up bowl all together – it will cause scratching. Avoid steel wool at all costs, since any wet fibres that remain in contact with the metal will cause rusting.

When buying cutlery with china, wooden or plastic handles, ask for advice about washing and polishing. Some handles may not react well to the heat of the dish-washing machine, so follow instructions carefully.

Polishing cutlery

Use a long term polish on silver or silver plate as it will stop tarnishing for quite a long period. For fork prongs that are difficult to clean, or handles with a carved or embossed pattern, use a silver dip. Silver polish is ideal for brightening pewter that has gone dull or tarnished. Pewter is generally very easy to keep clean and polished, as are bronze and gilded stainless steel. Never use silver polish on stainless steel. There are special preparations for stainless steel on the market.

Table mats

Fabric mats should be washed according to the manufacturer's instructions. Dry and iron carefully, using a little spray starch for cotton or linen mats, making sure that the fabric is stretched to a correct square or rectangle.

Lace needs very careful washing, either by hand or, if washed in a machine, inside a linen pillow case. Iron cotton lace from the centre outwards and place more delicate lace between clean white tissue paper before ironing.

Solid, heat-proof mats should be cleaned immediately after use to remove any grease and food stains. Take great care not to wet the green baize or felt underside as this will probably come loose and gradually fall off once it has been in contact with water. Wipe the top carefully with a soapy sponge or cloth, then wipe dry and polish with a soft cloth.

Tables and chairs

When buying furniture, always ask for advice or obtain the manufacturer's guidance on how best to care for wood and other finishes.

Wood

Too much polishing may cause a build up of polish which has a dulling effect – thorough regular dusting is much more effective. Give wood an occasional application of good furniture wax after dust has been removed. Once wax polish has been applied, a hard rub with a soft cloth should be enough to bring up the shine.

Antique pine is usually sold with a good layer of wax but sometimes has a layer of sanding seal between the wood and the wax which gives some resistance to heat or fluids. Check when you buy whether this has been applied or not. Even if it has, do not put hot dishes or

Decorate a table cloth on a seasonal theme, such as home-made mistletoe leaves and berries for Christmas. These can be sewn on to the cloth and removed later. Make the berries from beads, table-tennis balls or round, white Christmas tree decorations, and use card or thick paper for the leaves.

leave pools of liquid on the surface. Always use heat-proof mats. Wax the wood regularly with a good quality furniture wax.

Modern pine is often painted with a coat of clear, heat-resistant polyurethane varnish and all this needs is a wipe to remove grease and dirt. If the pine is not treated with a heat-resistant varnish, always use heat-proof mats and never put wet, sticky or hot items straight on to the table. This rule applies to all wooden surfaces.

Teak and other oiled woods need a few drops of teak oil about three times a year.

Surfaces finished with French polish

If you take care of the surface, the shine of the French polish should last for many years. Every three months or so polish it with a little beeswax furniture polish. Any grease spots or spilt food should be wiped off with warm soapy water and then the surface dried thoroughly.

If you buy second-hand or antique furniture that has an old or worn French polished surface it is probably best to get a craftsman to apply a new surface.

Plastic, perspex and laminates

Plastic and perspex will benefit from an occasional polish with an ordinary household polish. Matt finishes on plastic are best left unpolished but wiped with a damp chamoise leather. Laminates only need wiping with a damp cloth.

Bamboo and canework

Real bamboo should be wiped with a clean damp cloth and dried carefully. Canework tends to collect dust and crumbs so vacuum it regularly with a special upholstery attachment. Sturdy chairs can be turned upside down and banged firmly to knock all the bits out. Do this in the garden or on to a dust sheet. Dirty cane can be washed with a slightly wet soapy cloth. Rinse soap off carefully and pat dry with an absorbent duster or towel.

Glass-topped tables

If there are a lot of food stains on the glass, remove with a damp, soapy cloth. Then wipe with a damp chamois leather, polishing afterwards with a soft duster. Spray glass cleaners are also very effective for removing grease and other marks, but tend to leave smears unless the glass is rubbed really hard with kitchen towel or a soft cloth.

Steel and chrome

Use suitable steel or chrome cleaners, but always follow the manufacturer's instructions.

Marble

Marble-topped tables should be cleaned by scouring with powdered borax and then washed with plain, warm water.

Vases

Whenever you throw out a flower arrangement always wash the vase or container thoroughly. Any bacteria left behind will cause fouling of the water during subsequent usage and shorten the life of the flowers. Plantholders and candleholders used in arrangements should also be very carefully scrubbed and dried.

Making table cloths and napkins

How to make a circular table cloth

The measurements you need when buying fabric for a circular cloth are: the diameter of the table plus twice the length of drop. So, for example, for a cloth to fit a table 50 cm (20 inches) in diameter and to have a drop of 70 cm (28 inches) the total measurements needed are 50 + 70 + 70 cm (20 + 28 + 28 inches) plus a hem allowance.

The amount of fabric you buy depends on the width of the material. It is obviously best if you can cut a perfect circle from one large piece of fabric. A cloth for the table above would need a piece of fabric 190 cm x 190 cm (76 x 76 inches), plus a hem allowance. But if wide material is not available you will first have to join the fabric into a square.

Sewing a square from the fabric

1. First measure the diameter of the table and the length of drop required.
2. Double the length of the drop and add on 2 cm (¾ inch) hem allowance (for each side) and 5 cm (2 inches) for seam allowances.
3. For our sample table, this would mean:
   50 + 70 + 70 + 2 + 2 + 5 cm = 199 cm
   (20 + 28 + 28 + ¾ + ¾ + 2 inches = 79½ inches)
4. For example, if you buy fabric 122 cm (approx. 48 inches) wide, you will need to buy material twice the length, i.e. 199 cm x 2, so that you can cut one central panel and two side panels. You will cut a central panel 122 cm (approx. 48 inches) wide by 194 cm (77½ inches) long. From the remaining fabric cut two panels, each 38·5 cm (15½ inches) wide by 194 cm (77½ inches) long.
5. Pin and stitch them on the wrong side of the fabric, on each side of the central panel using 1·25 cm (½ inch) seams. Press the seams flat.
6. When joined, your fabric should be a perfect square measuring 194 x 194 cm (77½ x 77½ inches).

Cutting the circle

1. Having made or bought a big square, fold the fabric into four and, if possible, pin into place on a hardboard surface.
2. Measure the full length you require: the diameter and the drop plus the hem allowance multiplied by 2.
3. Halve the total to get the radius of the circle. For the cloth above, the radius would be 97 cm (38¾ inches).
4. Take a piece of string and tie it to a pencil (or chalk).
5. Measure the radius along the string from the pencil and make a mark on the string at the exact point.
6. Hold the point and place it on the central point (A) of the fabric.
7. Keep the string taut and make a circular movement with the pencil from corner B to corner C, drawing a quarter circle on the fabric.
8. After you have drawn a quarter circle, cut out carefully holding all four layers firmly together. When opened out it will be a perfect circle.

Hemming and finishing

With lightweight and thin, smooth fabrics, make a double

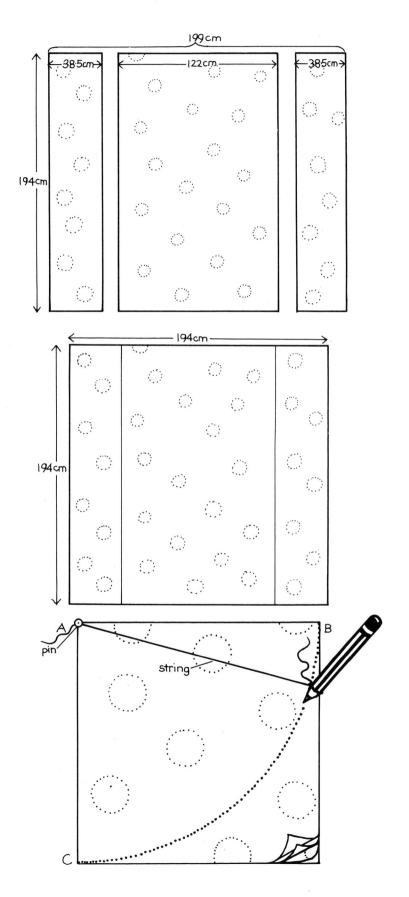

Making table cloths

A round table cloth should be cut from a square of fabric which can be made by joining widths of material. Instructions are given opposite. Here, widths are cut ready for joining to make a table cloth for a table 50 cm (20 inches) in diameter.

The panels of fabric are joined with 1·25 cm (½ inch) seams to make a perfect square. Join the panels selvedge to selvedge for neat seams.

The fabric is folded into four and a quarter circle is marked across the two edges which do not have folds.

hem by turning under 0·5 cm (approx. ¼ inch) then make a second turn of 1·5 cm (approx. ½ inch). Tack in place, then machine or hand hem all around the edge. Press flat.

With heavier fabrics, use braid or ribbon. Apply to the very edge of the right side of the cloth, turn in the width of the braid or ribbon and hem neatly.

Alternatively add the braid or ribbon, or a piece of lace, to the right side of the cloth and leave so that it shows as an extra detail to match the decor.

A rectangular or square cloth

The measurements you need to make a cloth for a rectangular or square cloth are:
● the length and width of the table, plus
● twice the drop at the end and twice the drop at the side.

For example, for a cloth to fit a table with a top measuring 125 x 90 cm (50 x 36 inches) and to have a drop of 60 cm (24 inches) all round, you need a piece of fabric measuring 245 cm (125 + 60 + 60 cm) x 210 cm (90 + 60 + 60 cm) (98 inches [50 + 24 + 24] x 84 inches [36 + 24 + 24]) plus 5 cm (2 inches) all round for hems making a grand total of 255 x 220 cm (102 x 88 inches).

You will probably have to join panels to make a cloth large enough, so work out the width that best suits the dimensions of your table. (For this table cloth buy fabric 122 cm (approx. 48 inches) wide and 510 cm (204 inches) long. Allow 2·5 cm (1 inch) for centre seam.
1. Cut two panels measuring 255 x 112.5 cm (102 x 45 inches) and sew a seam right down the middle.
2. Iron the seam flat. Make a neat hem all around the edge.

Join panels for a rectangular table cloth selvedge to selvedge

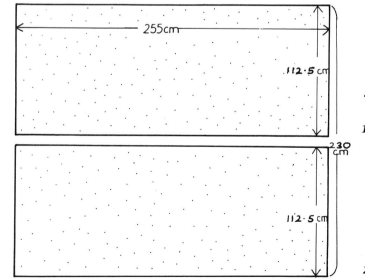

3. For lightweight fabrics make a double hem as for the circular table cloth. Machine or hand hem, taking care at the corners to fold the double layers of fabric neatly.
4. For heavier fabrics, make a single hem and use herringbone stitch – or use braid or binding tape. (See instructions for circular table cloth.)

Table napkins

To be sure of forming a perfect square or rectangle, cut a template from card or stiff paper. Use a set square to ensure that the corners are perfect right angles. Fold the fabric into two or four and cut two or four napkins at the same time.

When calculating how big to cut the napkins, remember that to make napkins which are big enough to fold into interesting shapes, you need a square at least 40 x 40 cm (16 x 16 inches), preferably bigger, plus a 2·5 cm (1 inch) hem allowance. They should be made of good quality linen. Hem napkins in the same way as table cloths.

Folding napkins

For decorative shapes you need starched, linen squares measuring at least 40 x 40 cm (16 x 16 inches). Smaller squares will not fold successfully. (To make small napkins attractive, tie with ribbons, roll into unusual or stylish napkin rings or fold into a triangle and let the colour scheme do the work.) Here are instructions for folding large, crisply starched squares into attractive and unusual shapes.

Candle

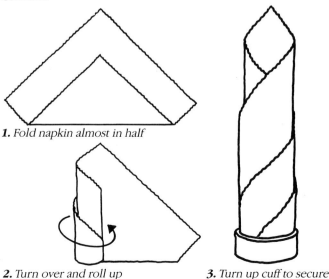

1. Fold napkin almost in half
2. Turn over and roll up
3. Turn up cuff to secure

140

Fan

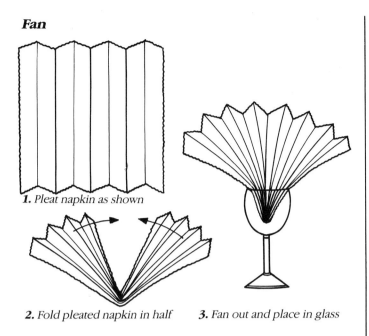

1. Pleat napkin as shown

2. Fold pleated napkin in half

3. Fan out and place in glass

Bishop's mitre

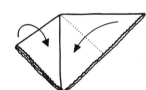

1. Fold napkin into triangle

2. Fold down two points as shown

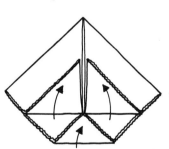

3. Fold back three points as shown

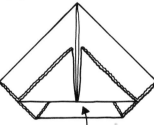

4. Fold over single point again

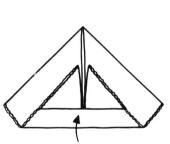

5. Fold over single point once more

6. Wrap wide points to back and tuck one inside the other to secure

Heart

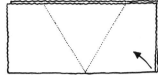

1. Fold napkin in half

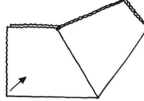

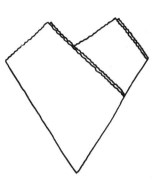

2. Bring lower right corner across, folding at dotted line

3. Repeat with left corner

Clown's hat

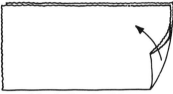

1. Fold in half and roll lower right corner towards centre top

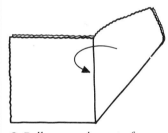

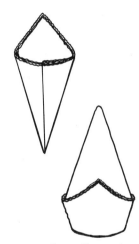

2. Roll over and over to form cone

3. Turn up hem all round

Lily

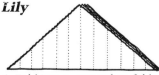

1. Fold into quarters then fold in half, points up, to form triangle. Pleat along dotted lines

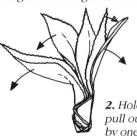

2. Hold at bottom and pull out 'petals' one by one

Rabbit

1. Fold in half, fold in half again, find centre

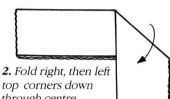

2. Fold right, then left top corners down through centre as shown

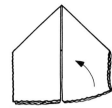

3. Fold bottom right raw edges up to rest on centre

5. Repeat procedure with left side

7. Tuck right point into left pocket

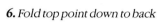

4. Fold right side point across to centre, central edges matching

6. Fold top point down to back

8. Turn up. Hey presto, a rabbit!

Sail boat

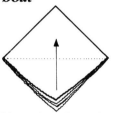

1. Fold into four, then fold all points up to form a triangle

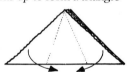

2. All points should be at top

3. Fold side points across and down through centre

4. Fold lower points up to back. Fold in half vertically

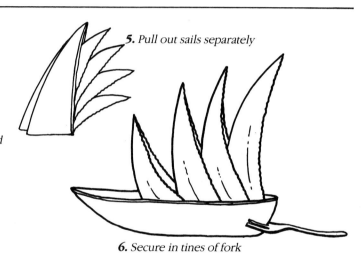

5. Pull out sails separately

6. Secure in tines of fork

Slipper or little boat

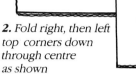

1. Fold napkin over and over into four. Find centre

2. Fold top right corner down through centre. Repeat at left

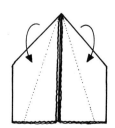

3. Fold top left corner downwards to centre. Repeat at right

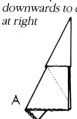

4. Fold sides together

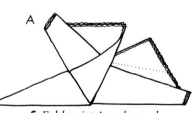

5. Fold point A under and through centre to be at right angles to centre

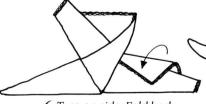

6. Turn on side. Fold back wing down as shown

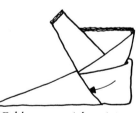

7. Fold extreme right point over and tuck it into flap as shown

8. Turn down cuff to complete slipper

Table setting techniques

Etiquette used to demand that the different items needed for eating and drinking be placed in a precise position according to very strict rules. Today, things are much more relaxed and flexible and there is no reason at all why implements shouldn't be placed where you like – within reason! The need for 'correctness' really depends on the formality of the occasion. For a traditional setting on a formal occasion it is usual to comply with the traditional guidelines. For everyday and informal meals it doesn't matter quite as much.

The general rules

Forks go on the left of the place settings and knives and spoons on the right. Guests should be able to tell, by working inwards, which implements to use for which course.

It is normal to place the side plate on the left and the glasses at the right-hand corner above the tips of the knife blades. If more than one wine is to be served, place the glasses in the order they will be used, working from left to right. The napkin can be placed on the side plate or on the mat or table cloth between the knives and forks. Forks should have the tips of the prongs pointing upwards, the knife blade should point inwards towards the table mat. Dessert spoons and forks can be placed at the side of the plate as in the illustration, or, to save space, above the plate for an informal setting. If fruit is served at the end of a meal it is usual to bring knives and forks to the table at the same time as the fruit bowl, and finger bowls if they are used.

Cutlery needed for hors d'oeuvres can be positioned ready with the course – for example a spoon for a prawn cocktail or a grapefruit, could be placed ready on the saucer or under-plate. In very formal settings such a course is placed on the table on top of the plates to be used for the subsequent courses. This causes problems as the plates cannot be heated. As it is preferable to have warm plates rather than a rigidly correct table setting, place hors d'oeuvre plates on another small plate if you feel they look lost without a background.

Acceptable variations

There is no reason why you shouldn't introduce originality to your table settings. Try placing knives and forks horizontally across rectangular mats; glasses in the middle of the space above the place setting instead of to

Place setting for a formal dinner

*Includes soup, fish course,
meat course, pudding, cheese
and biscuits*

Glasses

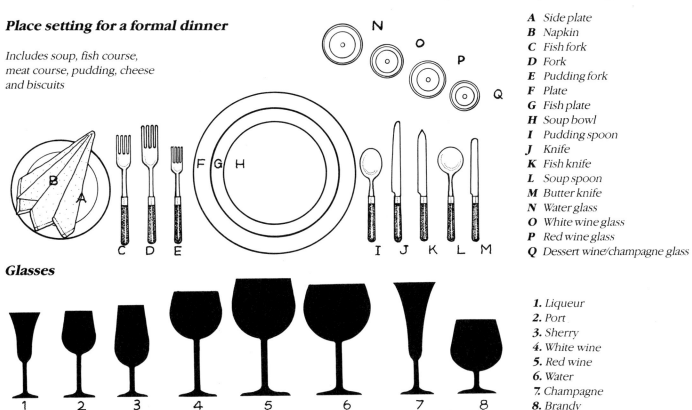

A Side plate
B Napkin
C Fish fork
D Fork
E Pudding fork
F Plate
G Fish plate
H Soup bowl
I Pudding spoon
J Knife
K Fish knife
L Soup spoon
M Butter knife
N Water glass
O White wine glass
P Red wine glass
Q Dessert wine/champagne glass

1. Liqueur
2. Port
3. Sherry
4. White wine
5. Red wine
6. Water
7. Champagne
8. Brandy

These menu cards have been made from thick silver card, placed in folded paper birds. Jewel eyes add the finishing touch. Origami, the Japanese art of paper-folding, could be used to make a great variety of figures to hold the cards – cats, dogs, rabbits, teddy bears, flowers, aircraft or whatever suits the theme of your table.

the right; rolled napkins in the space above the dessert spoons and forks; fork to the right of the place mat if the food demands a fork only or, for pasta, lay spoon and fork in a similar position. You may need to try new lay-outs to save space, or you may like to be unconventional. As long as the table looks attractive and guests have all they need, there shouldn't be many complaints!

Making place cards and menus

For simple, rectangular, stand-up name cards or menus, cut pieces of coloured card of a size to suit the table and table setting.

Cut out carefully and score the fold line with a blunt knife, knitting pin or similar instrument. To decorate

Keep the size in scale to the place card or menu you want to decorate. Cut out the stencil with a craft knife and push out the unwanted pieces. Trim with scissors or knife blade. Position the stencil over the card to be decorated and spray paint through the holes or apply with brushes.

How to make a border

Cut a piece of card slightly smaller than the place card or menu, and place carefully over it so that a regular border is still visible all round. Hold firmly in place and spray paint on to the exposed place card or menu or apply colour with a metallic felt-tip pen.

Writing the card or menu

For anyone who is not confident enough to write freehand, lettering sets are always useful, although the resulting print can look a little like a handout and the sets are quite slow and fiddly to use. Handwriting is better, and if done with felt-tip, a firm but flowing effect can be achieved. For a place card, position the name centrally in quite large writing but do not print in capitals. For a menu, write the date, and possibly the event, at the top, and then the different courses centrally positioned and evenly spaced under the title. Try to space the courses so that most of the card is filled. Decoration should flow around the edge or ornament the corners.

A picture frame is ideal for displaying the menu – but make sure that the menu fits the frame.

Novelty cards and menus

For children's parties it is fun to cut place cards and menus in the shape of a character or item to fit the theme – a clown's face, a train, a Father Christmas, a teddy bear, a cartoon character. First, find a piece of card that is white on one side and draw or trace the character or object on to the card – whatever size you need for a particular table.

Draw in the outlines with black felt-tip or Indian ink and fill in the colour with felt tip or paint. Make sure there is a large enough space for names or menus to be written in, and then leave to dry. Add any writing and cut the shape out. Press flat under a stack of books for a few hours, then, for a really shiny finish, paint or spray with a layer of varnish.

To stand the cards up, cut strong strips of thick card and mark fold lines in the centre. Score and bend. Apply a dab of glue to one end and stick to the back of the card so that the other end rests on the table.

the card either draw freehand designs in felt-tip, inks, or acrylic or poster paints or, for a more sophisticated look, cut a stencil to suit the theme of the table, and spray or stipple paint on to the card through the stencil.

How to make a stencil

Draw or trace your design on to a piece of firm cardboard.

145

Measurement plan for cracker

The measurement plan is essential in cracker-making. You will need to make a plan like the one here. This example has been scaled down but the proportions are correct. Use the exact measurements shown here. The plan can be made from fairly stiff white paper and marked with a felt-tip.

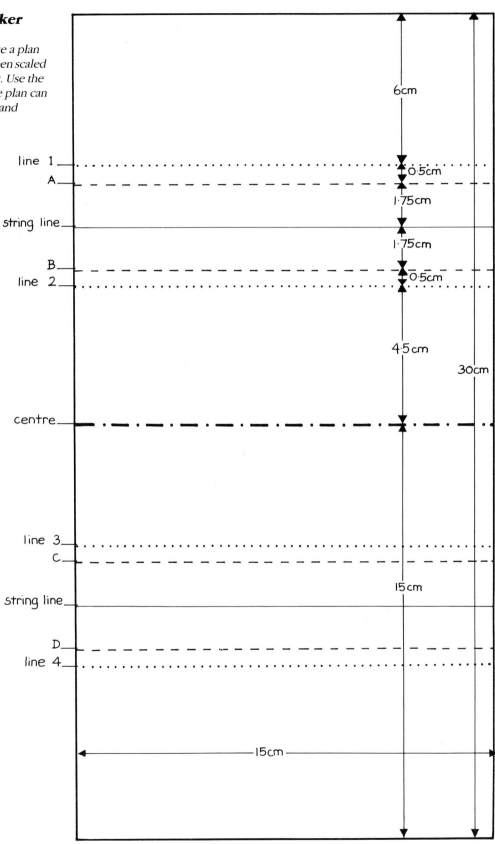

line 1

A

6cm

0·5cm

1·75cm

string line

1·75cm

B

0·5cm

line 2

4·5cm

30cm

centre

line 3

C

15cm

string line

D

line 4

15cm

Making crackers

Commercially produced crackers, or party favours as the Americans know them, are often so disappointing that you might prefer to make your own. They make a festive table even more special.

Basic materials

Lightweight card.
The 'snaps' or 'bangers'.
Strong string.
Strong glue.
Covering paper.
Small gifts for inside the cracker.
Formers or shapers made of metal and used for rolling the card to the required shape.

The basic materials should be available in novelty shops and good stationers. The card you use should be about the thickness of that used for cereal packets. The formers are sold in pairs, usually sizes 4 and 5. Size 4 makes a cracker 22 cm (8¾ inches) long and the tubes measure 20 cm (8 inches) and 10 cm (4 inches) long and 3·5 cm (1⅜ inches) in diameter.

Size 5 makes a cracker 27 cm (10¾ inches) long and the tubes are 25 cm (10 inches) and 12·5 cm (5 inches) long and 3·7 cm (1½ inches) in diameter.

If you don't want to buy these formers, cheaper alternatives are grey plastic piping used for household plumbing or aluminium tubing used for TV aerials.

For one cracker you need:
A snap or banger.
A motto or joke.
A gift.
A paper hat.
A piece of single crepe paper 30 x 17 cm (12 x 6¾ inches) with the grain running along the paper.
A piece of lining paper, 28 x 15 cm (11¼ x 6 inches).
A piece of stiffening card, 9 x 15 cm (3½ x 6 inches).
A pair of size 5 formers.

How to put your cracker together

1. Make a measurement plan marked out like the one here.
2. Take a piece of crepe paper and frill the ends by stretching them slightly.
3. Place the paper on top of the measurement plan.

4. Place the lining paper on top so that the edges nearest you match exactly (see below).

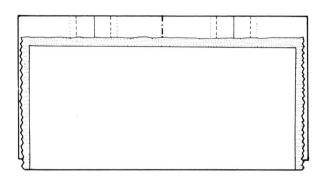

5. Place the banger and the joke or motto on top. Place the stiffening card in the centre so that the edges match the former lines 2 and 3 on your measurement plan.

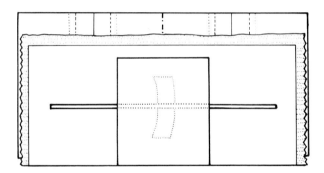

6. Apply some glue to the edge of crepe paper that can be seen behind the lining paper.
7. Place the longer former on top of the stiffener card so that one end is exactly in line with the stiffener card and about 2·5 cm (1 inch) from the edge of the paper nearest you.
8. Place the shorter former on to the paper so that its end touches the large former.

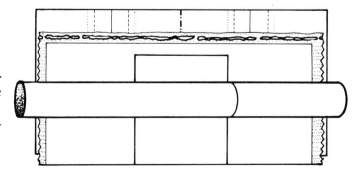

9. Carefully roll the crepe paper round the formers starting with the edge nearest to you. Keep the paper pressed as tightly as possible to the formers. When you reach the glued edge of crepe paper press the roll down firmly on to the glue and hold for half a minute so that it bonds firmly.

10. Move the entire roll slightly to the right so that the joint between the two formers is level with former line C on the plan.

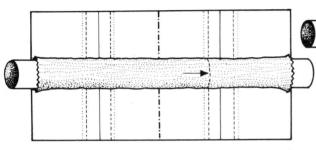

11. Gently pull the short former away from the longer one until its edge rests on former line D.

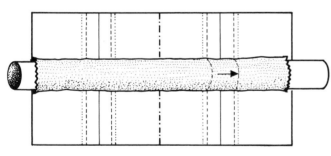

12. Place a piece of string under the roll along the string crease line. Place it twice round the cracker and then pull it tight.

13. Press the two formers back together and give a little twist to make a clean crease on the crepe paper. Remove the string and ease out the short former. Be careful that the long former stays in place.

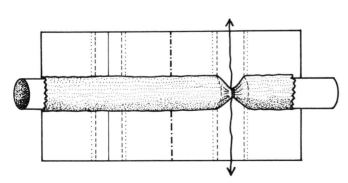

14. Lift up the cracker and drop in the gift and folded paper hat, then replace the cracker on the measurement plan.

15. Slide the former out making sure that the filling stays in position. Line the edge of the former with former line. The edge of the centre roll should be level with former line B.

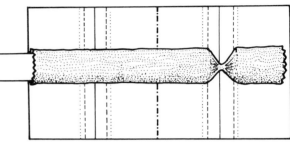

16. Twist the string carefully round the cracker along the other string crease line, being very careful not to crush the central roll which now has no support. Remove the string.

Ideas for gifts to go inside crackers

The contents of the cracker should be small and light but interesting or unusual. Here are some suggestions:

Packets of coloured drawing pins or paper clips	Hair ornaments – slides, clasps, combs etc.
Coloured adhesive tape	Coloured ribbons
Novelty pencil erasers	Earrings
Tiny notebooks or pencils	Beads
Short crayons or felt tips	Thimble
Watch strap	Ring
Small purse	Handkerchiefs
Novelty pencil sharpener	Tape measure
Tiny packs of playing cards	Novelty shoe laces
Emery boards	Sweets
Small nail brush	Matches
Small magnet	Tobacco
Travelling toothbrush	Small cigars or cigarettes
Films	Miniature toys
Pocket screwdriver	Wooden salt spoons
Tiny torch	Jar labels
Golf tees	Herb refills
Duster	Black peppercorns
Packets of seed	Nuts
Garden labels or ties	Pastry brush
Sewing threads	Cooking thermometer
Novelty key-ring	Jam pot covers

Decorating the cracker

If the paper you have chosen is very attractive or dramatic, you may not need or want to decorate it. If you feel it needs brightening, here are some ideas:

Bright bands of foiled paper glued at intervals round the cracker.

A solid band of perforated ribbon stuck round the central barrel.

Frills of crepe paper or brightly coloured paper attached carefully with strong glue around the ends of the cracker.

Cut-out shapes in bright foils stuck on to the barrel – make flowers, leaves, bells or abstract swirls – or make loops and rosettes from gift-wrap ribbon, to stick to the side of the cracker.

For children, numbers for birthdays can be glued to the sides or funny faces cut out and stuck to the ends.

A sprig of leaves or flowers attached to the barrel to complement any used in the centrepiece.

Garnishes and decorations

Attractive garnishes on dishes and plates of food give the perfect finishing touch to a beautifully set and decorated table. Large trays of food at a buffet table, little plates of hors d'oeuvres, dishes of vegetables, trays of sandwiches and cakes, dinner plates with fish or meat served ready, are all improved by a colourful, carefully made garnish. Try some of the following ideas:

Twists of lemon, orange, cucumber, lime or kiwi fruit These are suitable for decorating fish sandwiches, plates of vol au vents or canapés. Cut thin slices of unpeeled cucumber, lemon, orange, lime or peeled kiwi fruit. With a sharp knife, cut through to the middle of each slice. Twist the cut edges in opposite directions and lay on the food or plate.

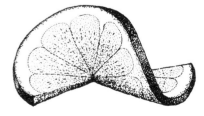

Cucumber or gherkin fans
Use these to decorate the edge of a plate or place directly on a steak or pork chop. You need a half slice of unpeeled cucumber approximately 1 cm (½ inch) thick or a whole

baby gherkin. With a sharp knife, cut almost through the entire piece three or four times. Cut from one tip but leave the other uncut. Splay the slices out and place on the food. The cucumber will look even more attractive if the skin is pared with a sharp peeler or paring implement first. Try the same with strawberries or apricot halves for decorating cakes and desserts.

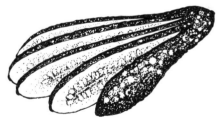

● **Radish roses**
These look beautiful resting at the side of a plate with parsley or mint leaves, or decorating a small tray of sandwiches or canapés. Wash the radish and trim off the stalk and top. Cut deeply into the radish forming 2 or 3 layers of petals. Soak in iced water and the petals will open out.

● Onion flowers

These look spectacular on a green salad or at the side of meat or fish. Peel and wash a small round onion. With a sharp knife cut radially through the onion to within 1 cm (½ inch) of the base. Make as many cuts as you can without separating the sections. Soak in iced water and from time to time gently curl the petals outwards and downwards.

● Tomato roses

Use these to decorate meat or fish dishes or fill gaps between sandwiches or canapés. Place watercress leaves or sprigs of mint underneath. Starting at the base of the tomato and using a sharp knife, peel off a continuous strip of skin approximately 1 cm (½ inch) wide. With the fleshy side in, curl the strip up tightly and set on the food.

● Turnip, white radish or carrot flowers

Peel a turnip, white radish or carrot and cut neat cross sections about 1 cm (½ inch) thick – thinner for carrots. Using a sharp pointed knife, cut the slice so that it has 5 or 6 petals. For the turnip or white radish flowers, cut a small circle of carrot for the middle and hold in place with a cocktail stick. For the carrot flowers, pipe a dot of cream cheese in the centre and fix in place a slice of olive or gherkin to form the centre of the flower. Use them to garnish any savoury dish.

● Spring onion curls

These look very delicate and are ideal for decorating Japanese or Chinese food. Peel and wash the onions and cut off the upper leaves. Make several cuts down the leaves to within 2·5 cm (1 inch) of the head. Soak in iced water and the leaves will curl beautifully.

● Grapes and cucumber slices on a cocktail stick

These make unusual decorations for fish or for plates of canapés or nibbles. Use seedless grapes and rings of cucumber slightly graduated in size. Push a cocktail stick through first a grape, then a slice of cucumber. Repeat twice more increasing the size of the slice of cucumber each time. Try the same effect with slices of lime or lemon and olives instead of grapes.

● Olive and cucumber twists

These look very attractive at the side of a plate of fish or sliced meat or as decoration for sandwiches. Using a vegetable peeler or very sharp knife, cut strips of cucumber peel and trim the edges and ends. Thread a cocktail stick through one end of the skin, then through an olive, then through the skin so that it forms a curve round the olive. Add another olive then go through the skin again. Repeat once or twice more. Try the same with neat strips of orange peel and black or green grapes. These would suit platefuls of sweet tartlets or little cakes.

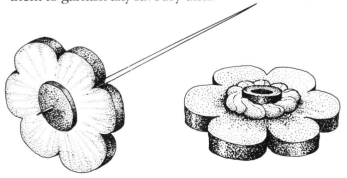

● Chocolate leaves

These are a perfect decoration for the top of a gâteau or trifle. Wash a regular shaped rose leaf and paint the underside with melted chocolate. Leave to dry, then paint with a second coat. When completely dry carefully peel off the leaf.

● Frosted fruits

Either in bunches or singly, these are useful for decorating trifles or cakes or to garnish a cheese board or dish of petits fours or chocolates. Wash and carefully dry such fruits as grapes, cherries, mandarin segments, redcurrants. Paint with beaten white of egg and dust with caster sugar. Leave on a sheet of greaseproof paper to dry thoroughly.

Decorating glass and china

Decorating glasses

There are times, such as cocktail parties or celebratory drinks, when drinking out of special, decorated glasses adds to the sense of occasion. But if such glasses aren't available it's possible to transform quite ordinary ones with an egg white and caster sugar decoration.

Beat the white of an egg until light and frothy, dip the rim of a clean glass into the egg and then into caster sugar. The result is a glittering crystalised rim. For a coloured variation, add a few drops of food colouring to the egg while beating. This colours the sugar that sticks to the egg.

You can also paint beaten egg white on to glasses in patterns or flowers. Dip a fine, sable hair paintbrush into beaten egg white and paint a design on to the glass. Paint quickly in small sections. Sprinkle with caster sugar, gently shake the excess sugar off and decorate the next section of the glass.

For a less sophisticated approach you can decorate glasses with butter icing. Beat icing sugar, food colouring and a little butter together to make butter icing. Pipe patterns or names around glasses or on to the base round the stem. This method can also be used to decorate paper cups at a children's party.

Decorating plates

To personalise china plates or to brighten up paper plates, try these ideas:
- ● Pipe butter icing in different colours around the rim or across the middle of plates. The icing can be removed or eaten before the plate is used. Pipe names or patterns or faces.
- ● Felt-tips (make certain that they are non-toxic) can be used to brighten up plain white paper plates, cups and tablecloths. Either do the decorating before the party or mealtime, or leave the children to do it during the meal.

Garnishing glasses

For cocktails and other drinks it is an attractive idea to decorate the glass. Here are some ideas:
- ● Cut rings of fruit (oranges, apple, lemon for example) and make a cut from the rind to the centre of each slice. Slide the cut over the rim of the glass. To keep the different slices of fruit together push half a cocktail stick through the slices. Conceal the ends of the stick

with an olive or cherry.

● Thread on to a cocktail stick some slices of lime alternated with maraschino cherries. Alternatively, use chunks of pineapple with strawberries or grapes.

● Slices of cucumber curved into a semicircle and

threaded on to a cocktail stick, around a cherry or grape, is an eye-catching garnish for gin based drinks or fruit punches.

● Rest a stick of celery, taken from the middle of the head, in a glass of Bloody Mary or fruit cocktail, so that

Garnishes add the finishing touch to any dish. Here, a sprinkling of grated cheese, cubes of crab meat, a liberal serving of chocolate sauce and angelica, even the rose petals scattered on the table cloth are thoughtful yet simple additions. Don't forget to garnish glasses also, in this case with a slice of lime and a redcurrant.

● Drape a sprig of redcurrants or blackcurrants over the edge of a glass of punch, martini or brandy cocktail.

Novelty ice cubes

To decorate drinks and bowls of punch or dishes of seafood, it is fun to make novelty ice cubes that are decorations in themselves.

For colour, add a few drops of food colouring to the water that is to be frozen. The cubes can be made to tone with the overall colour scheme.

Ice cubes can be made with flowers, mint leaves, herbs, sliced vegetables or fruit inside the ice. To do this, half fill the ice tray and freeze. When the water is solid, lay the flower head, fruit, herb or sliced vegetable to be frozen carefully into each cube. Slowly fill the ice tray with cold water and return to the freezer. It's sometimes difficult to get leaves, flowers and fruits to stay down in the water so that they freeze in the centre of the ice cube and not at the top. To ensure that they stay in the centre of the cube, half fill each compartment and place the items to be frozen into each one. Put the ice tray into the freezer. At the same time place a jug of water in the 'fridge. When the ice cubes are frozen remove them from the freezer and carefully top-up each cube from the jug of cold water from the 'fridge. Return the ice tray to the freezer. When the ice has frozen you should have perfect fruit and flower ice cubes.

Choose flowers, fruits, leaves, herbs and vegetables that fit the colour theme, so that pink petals from a rose echo a pink theme, or strawberries or raspberries suit a fruit theme. For dishes of seafood, freeze stems of dill or tarragon. Fill a bowl with these pretty cubes and rest oysters or prawns on top. This is very useful and attractive for a buffet where food may be sitting for a while and needs to be kept fresh.

To keep butter or pots of cream cool and fresh, make rings or circles of decorated ice to sit underneath butter dishes. To make these, fill small ring moulds with water and flowers in the same way as for ice cubes, or half fill little ramekins with water and flowers or fruits, and freeze. Place these frozen shapes on a glass dish or plate and sit the butter dish on the ice.

the pale green leaves stand above the drink.
● Thread slices of apricot or peach, alternated with slices of lime and black grapes on to a cocktail stick and use to garnish wine based fizzes or slings, or champagne cocktails.

INDEX

PICTURE CREDITS

Templar Publishing would like to extend their grateful thanks to the following people who have so generously contributed their help and advice.

All illustrations by Jane Launchbury.
Photographic credits (*a* = above, *b* = below, *l* = left, *r* = right, *i* = inset):
Phil Babb: 84*r*, 106*r*.
Charles Barker Lyons Ltd/Crown Paints/Harrison Drape: 16.
The Anthony Blake Photo Library: 86*r*, 100, 126*b*, 132.
Michael Boys: 13, 14*l*, 26, 33, 50, 51, 52, 54, 61*a*, 62, 80, 93*r*, 99, 101, 104, 125*b*.
Richard Bryant: 24, 118.
Camera Press Ltd: 10, 22, 37*r*, 42, 78*a* & *b*, 82*l*, 84*l*, 85*r*, 90, 94, 97, 108, 111*r*, 114, 121, 126*a*.
Conran Design Group: 18, 28, 122*r*, 128.
Creative Tableware: 122*l*.
Dulux: 14*r*, 47*r*, 133.
Falken/Rosenthal: 112.
Falken-Verlag GmbH.: 35, 49*r*, 56, 63, 86*l*, 89, 102, 125*a*.
Sheila Fitzjones PR Consultancy 30*a* & *b* (ICTT Tableware), 31*b* (Divertimenti).
Housewares: 39*r*, 61*b*, 113*i*, 127.
Di Lewis: 95*r*.
'Luxaflex' Vertical Drapes: 19*r*.

La Maison de Marie-Claire: 40, 131*r* (Chabaneix/ Bayle); 88 (Chabaneix/Benard/Renault); 53, 109 (Chabaneix/Renault); 76, 76*i* (Girandeau/Postic); 152 (Lippmann/Bonnet); 21, 116 (Nicolas/Postic); 15, 36, 83, 92, 106*l*, 110, 119*r*, 123*r* (Pataut/Bayle); 38 (Rozes/Hirsch).
100 Idées· 123*l*, 130, 144 (Maltaverne/Faver), 134 (Duffas/Schoumacher), 137 (Schall/Faver).
Sally Ormston: 60.
Rosenthal: 31*a*.
Royal Doulton Ltd/Royal Crown Derby: 32, 81.
Welbeck Public Relations/Dulux: 23*i*, 25*r*, 48.
Elizabeth Whiting & Associates: 12, 17, 20*l*, 34, 44, 46, 55*r*, 57*r*, 59, 96, 98.

For all photographs on pp 64-75, Templar Publishing would like to thank the following people:
Photography by James Jackson.
Stylist Pip Kelly.
China loaned by Rosenthal China Ltd, 3 Abercorn Trading Estate, Bridgewater Rd, Alperton, Wembley, Middlesex.
Cutlery loaned by Thomas Goode and Co Ltd, 19 South Audley St, Grosvenor Sq, London W1Y 6BN.
Table top loaned by The Reject Shop, Tottenham Court Rd, London W1.